P9-CRG-855

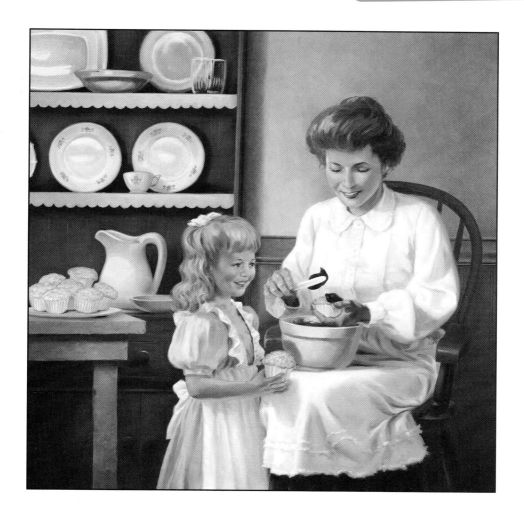

HERSHEY'S®

CLASSIC RECIPES™

Publications International, Ltd.
Favorite Brand Name Recipes at www.fbnr.com

Recipes, text and historical art copyright © 2000 Hershey Foods Corporation
Copyright © 2000 Publications International, Ltd.
All photographs *except* those on pages 99 and 101 copyright © Publications
International, Ltd.
All rights reserved. This publication may not be reproduced or quoted in whole or in part
by any means whatsoever without written permission from:

Louis Weber, CEO
Publications International, Ltd.
7373 North Cicero Avenue
Lincolnwood, Illinois 60712

Permission is never granted for commercial purposes.

HERSHEY'S, MINI KISSES, MINI CHIPS, REESE'S and SKOR are registered
trademarks of Hershey Foods Corporation, Hershey, PA 17033. MOUNDS is a licensed
trademark of Hershey Foods Corporation, Hershey, PA 17033.

Classic Recipes is a trademark of Publications International, Ltd.

Front cover illustration by Michael Jaroszko.

ISBN: 0-7853-8847-8

Library of Congress Catalog Card Number: 00-103271

Manufactured in China.

8 7 6 5 4 3 2 1

Microwave Cooking: Microwave ovens vary in wattage. Use the cooking times as
guidelines and check for doneness before adding more time.

Prep/Bake Times: Prep times are based on the approximate amount of time required to
assemble the recipe before baking, cooking, chilling or serving. These times include steps
such as measuring and mixing.

Table of Contents

Cookie Jar Favorites

Who can resist the aroma of fresh-baked cookies wafting through the house? Whatever recipe you choose, you're sure to please family and friends with these chocolate-filled delights.

Chocolate Chips and Raspberry Bars

$1^{1}/_{2}$ cups all-purpose flour

$^{1}/_{2}$ cup sugar

$^{1}/_{2}$ teaspoon baking powder

$^{1}/_{2}$ teaspoon salt

$^{1}/_{2}$ cup (1 stick) butter or margarine, softened

1 egg, beaten

$^{1}/_{4}$ cup milk

$^{1}/_{4}$ teaspoon vanilla extract

$^{3}/_{4}$ cup raspberry preserves

1 cup HERSHEY'S Semi-Sweet Chocolate Chips

1. Heat oven to 400°F. Grease 13×9×2-inch baking pan.

2. Stir together flour, sugar, baking powder and salt in large bowl. Cut in butter with pastry blender until mixture resembles coarse crumbs. Add egg, milk and vanilla; beat on medium speed of electric mixer until well blended.

3. Reserve $^{1}/_{2}$ cup mixture for topping. Spread remaining mixture onto bottom of prepared pan (this will be a very thin layer). Spread preserves evenly over dough; sprinkle chocolate chips over top. Drop reserved dough by $^{1}/_{2}$ teaspoons over chips.

4. Bake 25 minutes or until golden. Cool completely in pan on wire rack. Cut into bars.   *Makes about 32 bars*

Tip: Rich, buttery bar cookies and brownies freeze extremely well. Freeze in airtight containers or freezer bags for up to three months. Thaw at room temperature.

Hershey's "Perfectly Chocolate" Chocolate Chip Cookies

2¼ cups all-purpose flour

⅓ cup HERSHEY'S Cocoa

1 teaspoon baking soda

½ teaspoon salt

1 cup (2 sticks) butter or margarine, softened

¾ cup granulated sugar

¾ cup packed light brown sugar

1 teaspoon vanilla extract

2 eggs

2 cups (12-ounce package) HERSHEY'S Semi-Sweet Chocolate Chips

1 cup chopped nuts (optional)

1. Heat oven to 375°F.

2. Stir together flour, cocoa, baking soda and salt. Beat butter, granulated sugar, brown sugar and vanilla in large bowl on medium speed of electric mixer until creamy. Add eggs; beat well. Gradually add flour mixture, beating until well blended. Stir in chocolate chips and nuts, if desired. Drop by rounded teaspoons onto ungreased cookie sheet.

3. Bake 8 to 10 minutes or until set. Cool slightly; remove from cookie sheet to wire rack. *Makes about 5 dozen cookies*

Hershey's "Perfectly Chocolate" Chocolate Chip Cookies

Five Layer Bars

$3/4$ cup ($1^1/2$ sticks) butter or margarine
$1^3/4$ cups graham cracker crumbs
$1/4$ cup HERSHEY'S Cocoa
2 tablespoons sugar
1 can (14 ounces) sweetened condensed milk (not evaporated milk)
1 cup HERSHEY'S Semi-Sweet Chocolate Chips
1 cup raisins, chopped dried apricots or miniature marshmallows
1 cup chopped nuts

1. Heat oven to 350°F. Place butter in 13×9×2-inch baking pan. Heat in oven until melted. Remove pan from oven.

2. Stir together graham cracker crumbs, cocoa and sugar; sprinkle evenly over butter. Pour sweetened condensed milk evenly over crumb mixture. Sprinkle with chocolate chips and raisins. Sprinkle nuts on top; press down firmly.

3. Bake 25 to 30 minutes or until lightly browned. Cool completely in pan on wire rack. Cover with foil; let stand at room temperature 6 to 8 hours. Cut into bars.   *Makes about 36 bars*

Variation: Substitute 1 cup REESE'S Peanut Butter Chips for chocolate chips. Sprinkle 1 cup golden raisins or chopped dried apricots over chips. Proceed as above.

Cocoa Kiss Cookies

    1 cup (2 sticks) butter or margarine, softened
  $^2/_3$ cup granulated sugar
    1 teaspoon vanilla extract
 1$^2/_3$ cups all-purpose flour
  $^1/_4$ cup HERSHEY'S Cocoa
    1 cup finely chopped pecans
    1 bag (9 ounces) HERSHEY'S KISSES Milk Chocolates
       Powdered sugar

1. Beat butter, granulated sugar and vanilla in large bowl until creamy. Stir together flour and cocoa; gradually add to butter mixture, beating until blended. Add pecans; beat until well blended. Refrigerate dough about 1 hour or until firm enough to handle.

2. Heat oven to 375°F. Remove wrappers from chocolate pieces. Mold scant tablespoon of dough around each chocolate piece, covering completely. Shape into balls. Place on ungreased cookie sheet.

3. Bake 10 to 12 minutes or until set. Cool slightly, about 1 minute; remove from cookie sheet to wire rack. Cool completely. Roll in powdered sugar. Roll in sugar again just before serving, if desired.

Makes about 4$^1/_2$ dozen cookies

Hershey's Great American Chocolate Chip Cookies

1 cup (2 sticks) butter, softened
³/₄ cup granulated sugar
³/₄ cup packed light brown sugar
1 teaspoon vanilla extract
2 eggs
2¹/₄ cups all-purpose flour
1 teaspoon baking soda
¹/₂ teaspoon salt
2 cups (12-ounce package) HERSHEY'S Semi-Sweet Chocolate Chips
1 cup chopped nuts (optional)

1. Heat oven to 375°F.

2. Beat butter, granulated sugar, brown sugar and vanilla in large mixer bowl until creamy. Add eggs; beat well. Stir together flour, baking soda and salt; gradually add to butter mixture, beating well. Stir in chocolate chips and nuts, if desired. Drop dough by rounded teaspoons onto ungreased cookie sheet.

3. Bake 8 to 10 minutes or until lightly browned. Cool slightly; remove from cookie sheet to wire rack. Cool completely.

Makes about 6 dozen cookies

Hershey's Great American Chocolate Chip Pan Cookies: Spread dough into greased 15¹/₂×10¹/₂×1-inch jelly-roll pan. Bake at 375°F for 20 minutes or until lightly browned. Cool completely in pan on wire rack. Cut into bars. Makes about 48 bars.

12

Skor & Chocolate Chip Cookies: Omit 1 cup HERSHEY'S Semi-Sweet Chocolate Chips and nuts; replace with 1 cup finely chopped SKOR bars. Drop onto cookie sheets and bake as directed.

Great American Ice Cream Sandwiches: Prepare cookies as directed. Place one small scoop slightly softened vanilla ice cream between flat sides of two cookies. Gently press together. Wrap and freeze.

Top to bottom: Cocoa Kiss Cookies (page 11), Hershey's Great American Chocolate Chip Cookies

Rich Chocolate Chip Toffee Bars

2^1/$_3$ cups all-purpose flour

^{2}/$_3$ cup packed light brown sugar

^{3}/$_4$ cup (1^1/$_2$ sticks) butter or margarine

1 egg, slightly beaten

2 cups (12-ounce package) HERSHEY'S Semi-Sweet Chocolate Chips, divided

1 cup coarsely chopped nuts

1 can (14 ounces) sweetened condensed milk (not evaporated milk)

1^3/$_4$ cups (10-ounce package) SKOR English Toffee Bits, divided

1. Heat oven to 350°F. Grease 13×9×2-inch baking pan.

2. Stir together flour and brown sugar in large bowl. Cut in butter with pastry blender until mixture resembles coarse crumbs. Add egg; mix well. Stir in 1^1/$_2$ cups chocolate chips and nuts. Reserve 1^1/$_2$ cups mixture. Press remaining crumb mixture onto bottom of prepared pan.

3. Bake 10 minutes. Pour sweetened condensed milk evenly over hot crust. Top with 1^1/$_2$ cups toffee bits. Sprinkle reserved crumb mixture and remaining ^{1}/$_2$ cup chips over top.

4. Bake 25 to 30 minutes or until golden brown. Sprinkle with remaining ^{1}/$_4$ cup toffee bits. Cool completely in pan on wire rack. Cut into bars.

Makes about 36 bars

Rich Chocolate Chip Toffee Bars

Fudgey German Chocolate Sandwich Cookies

1 3/4 cups all-purpose flour

1 1/2 cups sugar

3/4 cup (1 1/2 sticks) butter or margarine, softened

2/3 cup HERSHEY'S Cocoa or HERSHEY'S Dutch Processed Cocoa

3/4 teaspoon baking soda

1/4 teaspoon salt

2 eggs

2 tablespoons milk

1 teaspoon vanilla extract

1/2 cup finely chopped pecans

Coconut and Pecan Filling (recipe follows)

1. Heat oven to 350°F.

2. Combine flour, sugar, butter, cocoa, baking soda, salt, eggs, milk and vanilla in large bowl. Beat at medium speed of electric mixer until blended (batter will be stiff). Stir in pecans.

3. Form batter into 1 1/4-inch balls. Place on ungreased cookie sheet; flatten slightly.

4. Bake 9 to 11 minutes or until almost set. Cool slightly; remove from cookie sheet to wire rack. Cool completely. Spread about 1 heaping tablespoon Coconut and Pecan Filling onto bottom of one cookie. Top with second cookie to make sandwich. Serve warm or at room temperature. *Makes about 17 sandwich cookies*

Coconut and Pecan Filling

$^1/_2$ cup (1 stick) butter or margarine
$^1/_2$ cup packed light brown sugar
$^1/_4$ cup light corn syrup
   1 cup MOUNDS Sweetened Coconut Flakes, toasted*
   1 cup finely chopped pecans
   1 teaspoon vanilla extract

*To toast coconut: Heat oven to 350°F. Spread coconut in even layer on baking sheet. Bake 6 to 8 minutes, stirring occasionally, until golden.

Melt butter in medium saucepan over medium heat; add brown sugar and corn syrup. Stir constantly, until thick and bubbly. Remove from heat; stir in coconut, pecans and vanilla. Use warm.   *Makes about 2 cups filling*

Peanut Butter Chip Triangles

1 1/2 cups all-purpose flour

1/2 cup packed light brown sugar

1/2 cup (1 stick) cold butter or margarine

1 2/3 cups (10-ounce package) REESE'S Peanut Butter Chips, divided

1 can (14 ounces) sweetened condensed milk (not evaporated milk)

1 egg, slightly beaten

1 teaspoon vanilla extract

3/4 cup chopped walnuts

Powdered sugar (optional)

1. Heat oven to 350°F. Stir together flour and brown sugar in medium bowl. Cut in butter with pastry blender or fork until mixture resembles coarse crumbs. Stir in 1/2 cup peanut butter chips. Press mixture into bottom of ungreased 13×9×2-inch baking pan. Bake 15 minutes.

2. Meanwhile, combine sweetened condensed milk, egg and vanilla in large bowl. Stir in remaining chips and walnuts. Spread evenly over hot baked crust.

3. Bake 25 minutes or until golden brown. Cool completely in pan on wire rack. Cut into 2- or 2 1/2-inch squares; cut squares diagonally into triangles. Sift powdered sugar over top, if desired.

Makes 24 or 40 triangles

Tip: To sprinkle powdered sugar over brownies, bars, cupcakes or other desserts, place sugar in a wire mesh strainer. Hold over top of desserts and gently tap sides of strainer.

Peanut Butter Chip Triangles

Oatmeal Butterscotch Cookies

$^3/_4$ cup (1$^1/_2$ sticks) butter or margarine, softened

$^3/_4$ cup granulated sugar

$^3/_4$ cup packed light brown sugar

2 eggs

1 teaspoon vanilla extract

1$^1/_4$ cups all-purpose flour

1 teaspoon baking soda

$^1/_2$ teaspoon salt

$^1/_2$ teaspoon ground cinnamon

3 cups quick-cooking or regular rolled oats, uncooked

1$^2/_3$ cups (10-ounce package) HERSHEY'S Butterscotch Chips

1. Heat oven to 375°F.

2. Beat butter, granulated sugar and brown sugar in large bowl until well blended. Add eggs and vanilla; blend thoroughly. Stir together flour, baking soda, salt and cinnamon; gradually add to butter mixture, beating until well blended. Stir in oats and butterscotch chips; mix well. Drop by teaspoons onto ungreased cookie sheet.

3. Bake 8 to 10 minutes or until golden brown. Cool slightly; remove from cookie sheet to wire rack. Cool completely.

Makes about 4 dozen cookies

Oatmeal Butterscotch Cookies

Filled Chocolate Bars

$^1/_4$ cup ($^1/_2$ stick) butter or margarine
1 square (1 ounce) HERSHEY'S Unsweetened Baking Chocolate,
    broken into pieces
1 egg
$^1/_2$ cup sugar
$^1/_4$ cup all-purpose flour
$^1/_8$ teaspoon salt
$^1/_2$ teaspoon vanilla extract
$^1/_2$ cup finely chopped almonds
    Vanilla Filling (recipe follows)
    Chocolate Chip Glaze (recipe follows)
    Sliced almonds

1. Heat oven to 400°F. Line 9-inch square baking pan with foil; grease foil.

2. Melt butter; immediately add chocolate; stir until chocolate is melted and mixture is smooth when stirred.

3. Beat egg in small bowl; add sugar, flour and salt, beating until well blended. Add chocolate mixture and vanilla; blend well. Stir in chopped almonds. Spread batter evenly in prepared pan.

4. Bake 10 to 12 minutes or until cake begins to pull away from sides; cool completely. Invert pan onto cutting board; peel off foil. Cut cake in half.

5. Spread one-half of cake with Vanilla Filling; top with remaining half. Spread Chocolate Chip Glaze on top; sprinkle with sliced almonds. Cut into bars. *Makes about 1 dozen bars*

Vanilla Filling: Combine $^1/_2$ cup powdered sugar, 1 tablespoon softened butter, $1^1/_2$ teaspoons milk and $^1/_4$ teaspoon vanilla extract in small bowl; beat to spreading consistency.

Chocolate Chip Glaze: Heat 2 tablespoons sugar and 1 tablespoon water to boiling in small saucepan. Remove from heat; immediately add $^1/_4$ cup HERSHEY'S Semi-Sweet Chocolate Chips, stirring until chips are melted and mixture is smooth. Use immediately.

Cocoa-Chip Cookies

$^2/_3$ cup shortening

$1^1/_2$ cups sugar

2 eggs

$^2/_3$ cup dairy sour cream

1 teaspoon vanilla extract

2 cups all-purpose flour

$^1/_2$ cup HERSHEY'S Cocoa or HERSHEY'S Dutch Processed Cocoa

$^1/_2$ teaspoon baking soda

$^1/_2$ teaspoon salt

2 cups (12-ounce package) HERSHEY'S MINI CHIPS Semi-Sweet Chocolate

1. Heat oven to 375°F. Lightly grease cookie sheet. Beat shortening and sugar in large bowl until blended. Add eggs, sour cream and vanilla; beat well. Stir together flour, cocoa, baking soda and salt; gradually add to shortening mixture, beating until well blended. Stir in small chocolate chips. Drop by teaspoons onto prepared cookie sheet.

2. Bake 8 to 10 minutes or until puffed and slightly cracked. Cool completely on wire rack. *Makes about $5^1/_2$ dozen cookies*

Almond Fudge Topped Shortbread

1 cup (2 sticks) butter or margarine, softened
$^1/_2$ cup powdered sugar
$^1/_4$ teaspoon salt
1 $^1/_4$ cups all-purpose flour
1 (12-ounce) package HERSHEY'S Semi-Sweet Chocolate Chips
1 (14-ounce) can sweetened condensed milk (not evaporated milk)
$^1/_2$ teaspoon almond extract
Sliced almonds, toasted

1. Heat oven to 350°F.

2. Beat butter, sugar and salt in large bowl until fluffy. Add flour; mix well. With floured hands, press evenly into greased 13×9-inch baking pan.

3. Bake 20 to 25 minutes or until lightly browned.

4. Melt chocolate chips and sweetened condensed milk in heavy saucepan, over low heat, stirring constantly. Remove from heat; stir in extract. Spread evenly over baked shortbread. Garnish with almonds; press down firmly. Cool. Chill 3 hours or until firm. Cut into bars. Store covered at room temperature.   *Makes 24 to 36 bars*

Almond Fudge Topped Shortbread

Peanut Butter and Chocolate Cookie Sandwich Cookies

$^1/_2$ cup REESE'S Peanut Butter Chips

3 tablespoons plus $^1/_2$ cup (1 stick) butter or margarine, softened and divided

$1^1/_4$ cups sugar, divided

$^1/_4$ cup light corn syrup

1 egg

1 teaspoon vanilla extract

2 cups plus 2 tablespoons all-purpose flour, divided

2 teaspoons baking soda

$^1/_4$ teaspoon salt

$^1/_2$ cup HERSHEY'S Cocoa

5 tablespoons butter or margarine, melted

Additional sugar

About 2 dozen large marshmallows

1. Heat oven to 350°F. Melt peanut butter chips and 3 tablespoons softened butter in small saucepan over very low heat. Remove from heat; cool slightly.

2. Beat remaining $^1/_2$ cup softened butter and 1 cup sugar in large bowl until fluffy. Add corn syrup, egg and vanilla; blend thoroughly. Stir together 2 cups flour, baking soda and salt; add to butter mixture, blending well. Remove $1^1/_4$ cups batter and place in small bowl; with wooden spoon, stir in the remaining 2 tablespoons flour and peanut butter chip mixture.

3. Blend cocoa, remaining $^1/_4$ cup sugar and 5 tablespoons melted butter into remaining batter. Refrigerate both batters 5 to 10 minutes or until firm enough to handle. Roll each dough into 1-inch balls; roll in sugar. Place on ungreased cookie sheet.

4. Bake 10 to 11 minutes or until set. Cool slightly; remove from cookie sheet to wire rack. Cool completely. Place 1 marshmallow on flat side of 1 chocolate cookie. Microwave at MEDIUM (50%) 10 seconds or until marshmallow is softened; place a peanut butter cookie over marshmallow, pressing down slightly. Repeat for remaining cookies. Serve immediately.

Makes about 2 dozen sandwich cookies

Peanut Butter and Chocolate Cookie Sandwich Cookies

Chewy Rocky Road Bars

$1^{1}/_{2}$ cups finely crushed unsalted pretzels

$^{3}/_{4}$ cup ($1^{1}/_{2}$ sticks) butter or margarine, melted

1 can (14 ounces) sweetened condensed milk (not evaporated milk)

2 cups miniature marshmallows

1 cup HERSHEY'S Butterscotch Chips

1 cup HERSHEY'S Semi-Sweet Chocolate Chips

1 cup MOUNDS Sweetened Coconut Flakes

$^{3}/_{4}$ cup chopped nuts

1. Heat oven to 350°F.

2. Combine crushed pretzels and butter in small bowl; lightly press mixture into bottom of 13×9×2-inch baking pan. Pour sweetened condensed milk evenly over crumb mixture. Top with marshmallows, butterscotch chips, chocolate chips, coconut and nuts. Press toppings firmly into sweetened condensed milk.

3. Bake 25 to 30 minutes or until lightly browned. Cool completely in pan on wire rack. Cut into bars. *Makes about 36 bars*

Variations: 2 cups (12-ounce package) HERSHEY'S Semi-Sweet Chocolate Chips or $1^{2}/_{3}$ cups (10-ounce package) HERSHEY'S Butterscotch Chips may be used instead of 1 cup of each flavor.

— MADE ON THE FARM —

This Illustrates a real Cocoa pod right from the plantation, broken open, showing the natural Cocoa beans as used by the Hershey Chocolate Co., Hershey, Pa.

Chocolate Chip Caramel Nut Cookies

18 caramels, unwrapped
1 cup shortening
1 cup granulated sugar
$^1/_2$ cup firmly packed brown sugar
2 eggs, beaten
2$^3/_4$ cups all-purpose flour
1 teaspoon baking soda
1 teaspoon salt
1 teaspoon vanilla extract
$^1/_2$ teaspoon hot water
1 cup HERSHEY'S Semi-Sweet Chocolate Chips
$^1/_2$ cup coarsely chopped unsalted peanuts

1. Heat oven to 400°F.

2. Cut each caramel into 4 pieces. Cut each piece into 6 pieces.

3. Combine shortening, granulated sugar and brown sugar in large bowl. Beat at medium speed of electric mixer until well blended and creamy. Beat in eggs.

4. Combine flour, baking soda and salt. Add gradually to shortening mixture at low speed of electric mixer. Mix until well blended. Beat in vanilla and hot water. Stir in caramels, chocolate chips and nuts with spoon. Drop two slightly rounded tablespoons 3 inches apart onto ungreased cookie sheet for each cookie. Shape dough into circles, 2 inches in diameter and 1 inch high.

5. Bake 7 to 9 minutes or until light golden brown. Cool 5 minutes on cookie sheet before removing to wire rack.

Makes 2 to 2$^1/_2$ dozen cookies

Peanut Butter Chips and Jelly Bars

1 1/2 cups all-purpose flour

1/2 cup sugar

3/4 teaspoon baking powder

1/2 cup (1 stick) cold butter or margarine

1 egg, beaten

3/4 cup grape jelly

1 2/3 cups (10-ounce package) REESE'S Peanut Butter Chips, divided

1. Heat oven to 375°F. Grease 9-inch square baking pan.

2. Stir together flour, sugar and baking powder. With pastry blender, cut in butter until mixture resembles coarse crumbs. Add egg; blend well. Reserve half of mixture; press remaining mixture onto bottom of prepared pan. Spread jelly over crust. Sprinkle 1 cup peanut butter chips over jelly. Stir together reserved crumb mixture with remaining 2/3 cup chips; sprinkle over top.

3. Bake 25 to 30 minutes or until lightly browned. Cool completely in pan on wire rack. Cut into bars. *Makes about 16 bars*

Tip: For a whimsical twist on this tried-and-true classic, use cookie cutters to cut out shapes for added fun.

Top to bottom: Peanut Butter Chips and Jelly Bars, Best Brownies (page 46)

Three-in-One Chocolate Chip Cookies

6 tablespoons butter or margarine, softened

$^{1}/_{2}$ cup packed light brown sugar

$^{1}/_{4}$ cup granulated sugar

1 egg

1 teaspoon vanilla extract

1 $^{1}/_{2}$ cups all-purpose flour

$^{1}/_{2}$ teaspoon baking soda

$^{1}/_{4}$ teaspoon salt

2 cups (12-ounce package) HERSHEY'S Semi-Sweet Chocolate Chips

Beat butter, brown sugar and granulated sugar in large bowl until fluffy. Add egg and vanilla; beat well. Stir together flour, baking soda and salt; gradually blend into butter mixture. Stir in chocolate chips. Shape and bake cookies into one of the three versions below.

Giant Cookie: Prepare dough. Heat oven to 350°F. Line 12×$^{5}/_{8}$-inch round pizza pan with foil. Pat dough evenly into prepared pan to within $^{3}/_{4}$ inch of edge. Bake 15 to 18 minutes or until lightly browned. Cool completely; cut into wedges. Decorate or garnish as desired. Makes about 8 servings (one 12-inch cookie).

Medium-Size Refrigerator Cookies: Prepare dough. On wax paper, shape into 2 rolls, 1 $^{1}/_{2}$ inches in diameter. Wrap in wax paper; cover with plastic wrap. Refrigerate several hours, or until firm enough to slice. Heat oven to 350°F. Remove rolls from refrigerator; remove wrapping. With sharp knife, cut into $^{1}/_{4}$-inch-wide slices. Place on ungreased cookie sheet, about

3 inches apart. Bake 8 to 10 minutes or until lightly browned. Cool slightly; remove from cookie sheet to wire rack. Cool completely. Makes about 2$^1/_2$ dozen (2$^1/_2$-inch) cookies.

Miniature Cookies: Prepare dough. Heat oven to 350°F. Drop dough by $^1/_4$ teaspoons onto ungreased cookie sheet, about 1$^1/_2$ inches apart. (Or, spoon dough into disposable plastic frosting bag; cut about $^1/_4$ inch off tip. Squeeze batter by $^1/_4$ teaspoons onto ungreased cookie sheet.) Bake 5 to 7 minutes or just until set. Cool slightly; remove from cookie sheet to wire rack. Cool completely. Makes about 18$^1/_2$ dozen ($^3/_4$-inch) cookies.

Giant Three-in-One Chocolate Chip Cookie

Chocolate Thumbprint Cookies

$^1/_2$ cup (1 stick) butter or margarine, softened

$^2/_3$ cup sugar

1 egg, separated

2 tablespoons milk

1 teaspoon vanilla extract

1 cup all-purpose flour

$^1/_3$ cup HERSHEY'S Cocoa

$^1/_4$ teaspoon salt

1 cup chopped nuts

Vanilla Filling (recipe follows)

26 HERSHEY'S KISSES Milk Chocolates, HERSHEY'S HUGS Chocolates, pecan halves or candied cherry halves

1. Beat butter, sugar, egg yolk, milk and vanilla in medium bowl until fluffy. Stir together flour, cocoa and salt; gradually add to butter mixture, beating until blended. Refrigerate dough at least 1 hour or until firm enough to handle.

2. Heat oven to 350°F. Lightly grease cookie sheet. Shape dough into 1-inch balls. With fork, beat egg white slightly. Dip each ball into egg white; roll in nuts. Place on prepared cookie sheet. Press thumb gently in center of each cookie.

3. Bake cookies 10 to 12 minutes or until set. Meanwhile, prepare Vanilla Filling. Remove wrappers from chocolate pieces. Remove cookies from cookie sheet to wire rack; cool 5 minutes. Spoon about $^1/_4$ teaspoon prepared filling into each thumbprint. Gently press chocolate piece onto top of each cookie. Cool completely. *Makes about 2 dozen cookies*

Vanilla Filling

$^1/_2$ cup powdered sugar

1 tablespoon butter or margarine, softened

2 teaspoons milk

$^1/_4$ teaspoon vanilla extract

Combine powdered sugar, butter, milk and vanilla; beat until smooth.

Cocoa Crinkle Cookies

2 cups granulated sugar

$^3/_4$ cup vegetable oil

$^3/_4$ cup HERSHEY'S Cocoa

4 eggs

2 teaspoons vanilla extract

$2^1/_3$ cups all-purpose flour

2 teaspoons baking powder

$^1/_2$ teaspoon salt

Powdered sugar

1. Stir together granulated sugar and oil in large mixer bowl; add cocoa, blending well. Beat in eggs and vanilla. Stir together flour, baking powder and salt in separate bowl; add to cocoa mixture, blending well. Cover; refrigerate at least 6 hours.

2. Heat oven to 350°F. Grease cookie sheet.

3. Shape dough into 1-inch balls; roll in powdered sugar. Place 2 inches apart on prepared cookie sheet. Bake 12 to 14 minutes or until almost no indentation remains when touched. Remove from cookie sheet to wire rack. Cool completely. *Makes about 4 dozen cookies*

Irrestistible Brownies

Fudgey, rich, chunky, chewy brownies
are a true chocolate lover's dream.
Drizzled with caramel, studded with chips,
covered with frosting . . . . mmmmm.

Hershey's White Chip Brownies

4 eggs

1 1/4 cups sugar

1/2 cup (1 stick) butter or margarine, melted

2 teaspoons vanilla extract

1 1/3 cups all-purpose flour

2/3 cup HERSHEY'S Cocoa

1 teaspoon baking powder

1/2 teaspoon salt

1 2/3 cups (10-ounce package) HERSHEY'S Premier White Chips

1. Heat oven to 350°F. Grease 13×9×2-inch baking pan.

2. Beat eggs in large bowl until foamy; gradually beat in sugar. Add butter and vanilla; beat until blended. Stir together flour, cocoa, baking powder and salt; add to egg mixture, beating until blended. Stir in white chips. Spread batter into prepared pan.

3. Bake 25 to 30 minutes or until brownies begin to pull away from sides of pan. Cool completely in pan on wire rack. Cut into squares.

Makes about 36 brownies

Tip: Brownies and bar cookies cut into different shapes can add interest to a plate of simple square cookies. Cut cookies into different size rectangles, or make triangles by cutting the cookies into 2- to 2 1/2-inch squares; then cut each square in half diagonally. To make diamond shapes, cut straight lines 1 or 1 1/2 inches apart the length of the baking pan, then cut straight lines 1 1/2 inches apart diagonally across the pan.

P.B. Chips Brownie Cups

  1 cup (2 sticks) butter or margarine
  2 cups sugar
  2 teaspoons vanilla extract
  4 eggs
  ³/₄ cup HERSHEY'S Cocoa or HERSHEY'S Dutch Processed
       Cocoa
1 ³/₄ cups all-purpose flour
  ¹/₂ teaspoon baking powder
  ¹/₂ teaspoon salt
1 ²/₃ cups (10-ounce package) REESE'S Peanut Butter Chips,
       divided

1. Heat oven to 350°F. Line 18 muffin cups (2¹/₂ inches in diameter) with paper or foil bake cups.

2. Place butter in large microwave-safe bowl. Microwave at HIGH (100%) 1 to 1¹/₂ minutes or until melted. Stir in sugar and vanilla. Add eggs; beat well. Add cocoa; beat until well blended. Add flour, baking powder and salt; beat well. Stir in 1¹/₃ cups peanut butter chips. Divide batter evenly into muffin cups; sprinkle with remaining ¹/₃ cup peanut butter chips.

3. Bake 25 to 30 minutes or until surface is firm; cool completely in pan on wire rack.   *Makes about 1¹/₂ dozen brownie cups*

P.B. Chips Brownie Cups

Brownie Pie à la Mode

$^{1}/_{2}$ cup sugar

2 tablespoons butter or margarine

2 tablespoons water

1$^{1}/_{3}$ cups HERSHEY'S Semi-Sweet Chocolate Chips

2 eggs

$^{2}/_{3}$ cup all-purpose flour

$^{1}/_{4}$ teaspoon baking soda

$^{1}/_{4}$ teaspoon salt

1 teaspoon vanilla extract

$^{3}/_{4}$ cup chopped nuts (optional)

Fudge Sauce (recipe follows, optional)

Ice cream, any flavor

1. Heat oven to 350°F. Grease 9-inch pie plate.

2. Combine sugar, butter and water in medium saucepan. Cook over medium heat, stirring occasionally, just until mixture comes to a boil. Remove from heat. Immediately add chocolate chips; stir until melted. Add eggs; beat with spoon until well blended.

3. Stir together flour, baking soda and salt. Add to chocolate mixture; stir until well blended. Stir in vanilla and nuts, if desired; pour into prepared pie plate.

4. Bake 25 to 30 minutes or until almost set. (Pie will not test done in center.) Cool. Prepare Fudge Sauce, if desired. Top warm pie with scoops of ice cream and prepared sauce. *Makes 8 to 10 servings*

Fudge Sauce

1 cup HERSHEY'S Semi-Sweet Chocolate Chips
$^1/_2$ cup evaporated milk
$^1/_4$ cup sugar
1 tablespoon butter or margarine

Combine all ingredients in medium microwave-safe bowl. Microwave at HIGH (100%) 1 minute; stir. If necesssary, microwave at HIGH an additional 15 seconds at a time, stirring after each heating, just until chips are melted and mixture is smooth.

Quick & Easy Fudgey Brownies

4 bars (1 ounce each) HERSHEY'S Unsweetened Baking
    Chocolate, broken into pieces

³/₄ cup (1¹/₂ sticks) butter or margarine

2 cups sugar

3 eggs

1¹/₂ teaspoons vanilla extract

1 cup all-purpose flour

1 cup chopped nuts (optional)

Creamy Quick Chocolate Frosting (recipe follows, optional)

1. Heat oven to 350°F. Grease 13×9×2-inch baking pan.

2. Place chocolate and butter in large microwave-safe bowl. Microwave at HIGH (100%) 1¹/₂ to 2 minutes or until chocolate is melted and mixture is smooth when stirred. Add sugar; stir with spoon until well blended. Add eggs and vanilla; mix well. Add flour and nuts, if desired; stir until well blended. Spread into prepared pan.

3. Bake 30 to 35 minutes or until wooden pick inserted in center comes out almost clean. Cool in pan on wire rack.

4. Frost with Creamy Quick Chocolate Frosting, if desired. Cut into squares.   *Makes about 24 brownies*

Creamy Quick Chocolate Frosting

    3 tablespoons butter or margarine

    3 bars (1 ounce each) HERSHEY'S Unsweetened Baking
        Chocolate, broken into pieces

    3 cups powdered sugar

$^1/_2$ cup milk

    1 teaspoon vanilla extract

$^1/_8$ teaspoon salt

Melt butter and chocolate in saucepan over very low heat. Cook, stirring constantly, until chocolate is melted and mixture is smooth. Pour into large bowl; add powdered sugar, milk, vanilla and salt. Beat on medium speed of electric mixer until well blended. If necessary, refrigerate 10 minutes or until of spreading consistency.   *Makes about 2 cups frosting*

Quick & Easy Fudgey Brownies

Three Great Tastes Blond Brownies

2 cups packed light brown sugar

1 cup (2 sticks) butter or margarine, melted

2 eggs

2 teaspoons vanilla extract

2 cups all-purpose flour

1 teaspoon salt

$2/3$ cup (of each) HERSHEY'S Semi-Sweet Chocolate Chips, REESE'S Peanut Butter Chips, and HERSHEY'S Premier White Chips

Chocolate Chip Drizzle (recipe follows)

1. Heat oven to 350°F. Grease $15^1/_2 \times 10^1/_2 \times 1$-inch jelly-roll pan.

2. Stir together brown sugar and butter in large bowl; beat in eggs and vanilla until smooth. Add flour and salt, beating just until blended; stir in chocolate, peanut butter and white chips. Spread batter into prepared pan.

3. Bake 25 to 30 minutes or until wooden pick inserted in center comes out clean. Cool completely in pan on wire rack. Cut into bars. With tines of fork, drizzle Chocolate Chip Drizzle randomly over bars.

Makes about 72 bars

Chocolate Chip Drizzle: In small microwave-safe bowl, place $1/4$ cup HERSHEY'S Semi-Sweet Chocolate Chips and $1/4$ teaspoon shortening (do not use butter, margarine, spread or oil). Microwave at HIGH (100%) 30 seconds to 1 minute; stir until chips are melted and mixture is smooth.

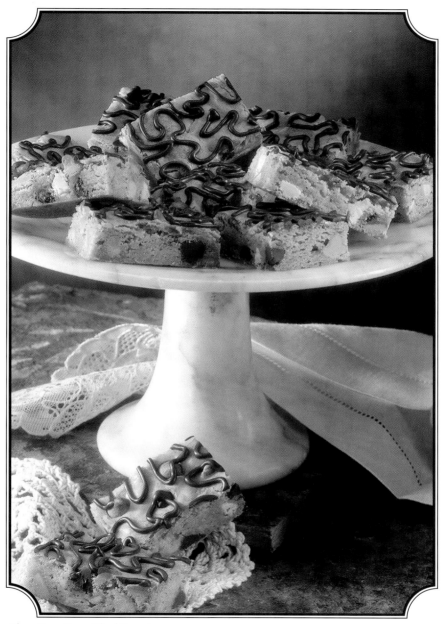

Three Great Tastes Blond Brownies

Best Brownies

$^{1}/_{2}$ cup (1 stick) butter or margarine, melted

1 cup sugar

1 teaspoon vanilla extract

2 eggs

$^{1}/_{2}$ cup all-purpose flour

$^{1}/_{3}$ cup HERSHEY'S Cocoa

$^{1}/_{4}$ teaspoon baking powder

$^{1}/_{4}$ teaspoon salt

$^{1}/_{2}$ cup chopped nuts (optional)

Creamy Brownie Frosting (recipe follows)

1. Heat oven to 350°F. Grease 9-inch square baking pan. Stir together butter, sugar and vanilla in large bowl. Add eggs; beat well. Combine flour, cocoa, baking powder and salt; gradually add to butter mixture, beating until well blended. Stir in nuts, if desired. Spread into prepared pan.

2. Bake 20 to 25 minutes or until brownies begin to pull away from sides of pan. Cool; frost with Creamy Brownie Frosting. Cut into squares.

Makes about 16 brownies

Creamy Brownie Frosting

3 tablespoons butter or margarine, softened

3 tablespoons HERSHEY'S Cocoa

1 tablespoon light corn syrup or honey

$^{1}/_{2}$ teaspoon vanilla extract

1 cup powdered sugar

1 to 2 tablespoons milk

Beat butter, cocoa, corn syrup and vanilla. Add powdered sugar and milk; beat to spreading consistency.

Makes about 1 cup frosting

Double Chocolate Brownie Bars

$^1/_2$ cup (1 stick) butter or margarine

2 cups (12-ounce package) HERSHEY'S Semi-Sweet Chocolate Chips, divided

$1^1/_2$ cups sugar

$1^1/_4$ cups all-purpose flour

3 eggs

1 teaspoon vanilla extract

$^1/_2$ teaspoon baking powder

$^1/_2$ teaspoon salt

1 cup coarsely chopped walnuts

1. Heat oven to 350°F. Grease 13×9×2-inch baking pan.

2. Place butter and 1 cup chocolate chips in large microwave-safe bowl. Microwave at HIGH (100%) 1 to $1^1/_2$ minutes or until chips are melted when stirred. Add sugar, flour, eggs, vanilla, baking powder and salt; stir with spoon until smooth. Stir in remaining 1 cup chips. Spread batter into prepared pan; sprinkle walnuts over top.

3. Bake 30 minutes or until center is set. Cool completely in pan on wire rack. Cut into bars. Store tightly covered.   *Makes about 36 brownies*

Variation: Cut brownies into 3×3$^1/_4$-inch squares. Serve topped with scoops of ice cream, fruit and chocolate syrup.

Brownie Caramel Pecan Bars

$^1/_2$ cup sugar

2 tablespoons butter or margarine

2 tablespoons water

2 cups (12-ounce package) HERSHEY'S Semi-Sweet Chocolate
   Chips, divided

2 eggs

1 teaspoon vanilla extract

$^2/_3$ cup all-purpose flour

$^1/_4$ teaspoon baking soda

$^1/_4$ teaspoon salt

   Caramel Topping (recipe follows)

1 cup pecan pieces

1. Heat oven to 350°F. Line 9-inch square baking pan with foil, extending foil over edges of pan. Grease and flour foil.

2. In medium saucepan, combine sugar, butter and water; cook over low heat, stirring constantly, until mixture boils. Remove from heat. Immediately add 1 cup chocolate chips; stir until melted. Beat in eggs and vanilla until well blended. Stir together flour, baking soda and salt; stir into chocolate mixture. Spread batter into prepared pan.

3. Bake 15 to 20 minutes or until brownies begin to pull away from sides of pan. Meanwhile, prepare Caramel Topping. Remove brownies from oven; immediately and carefully spread with prepared topping. Sprinkle remaining 1 cup chips and pecans over topping. Cool completely in pan on wire rack, being careful not to disturb chips while soft. Lift out of pan. Cut into bars.   *Makes about 16 bars*

Caramel Topping: Remove wrappers from 25 caramels. In medium microwave-safe bowl, place ¼ cup (½ stick) butter or margarine, caramels and 2 tablespoons milk. Microwave at HIGH (100%) 1 minute; stir. Microwave an additional 1 to 2 minutes, stirring every 30 seconds, or until caramels are melted and mixture is smooth when stirred. Use immediately.

Brownie Caramel Pecan Bars

Miniature Brownie Cups

6 tablespoons butter or margarine, melted

$^3/_4$ cup sugar

$^1/_2$ teaspoon vanilla extract

2 eggs

$^1/_2$ cup all-purpose flour

$^1/_4$ cup HERSHEY'S Cocoa or HERSHEY'S Dutch Processed Cocoa

$^1/_4$ teaspoon baking powder

Dash salt

$^1/_4$ cup finely chopped nuts

1. Heat oven to 350°F. Line small muffin cups ($1^3/_4$ inches in diameter) with paper bake cups. Stir together butter, sugar and vanilla in medium bowl. Add eggs; beat well with spoon.

2. Stir together flour, cocoa, baking powder and salt; gradually add to butter mixture, beating with spoon until well blended. Fill muffin cups $^1/_2$ full with batter; sprinkle nuts over top.

3. Bake 12 to 15 minutes or until wooden pick inserted in center comes out almost clean. Cool slightly; remove brownies from pan to wire rack. Cool completely. *Makes about 24 brownies*

Tip: HERSHEY'S Dutch Processed Cocoa involves a process which neutralizes the natural acidity found in cocoa powder. This results in a darker cocoa with a more mellow flavor than natural cocoa.

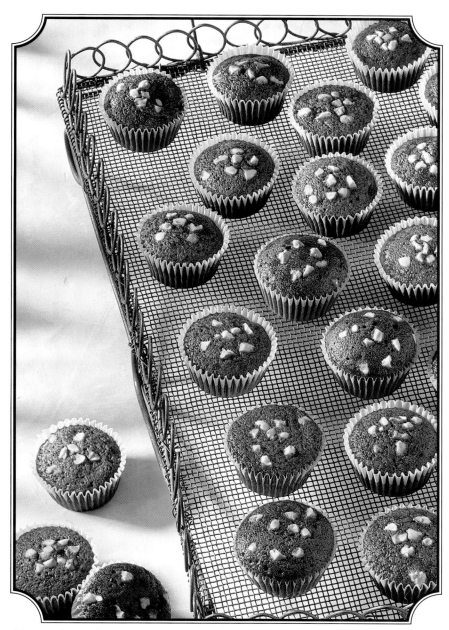

Miniature Brownie Cups

Collectible Cakes & More

Here are the tried-and-true classics from
the Hershey Kitchens—beautiful to look
at and even better to eat. Layer cakes,
cheesecakes, tortes and pies make
unforgettable endings to any meal.

Chocolate Cherry Cream-Filled Log

4 eggs, separated

$^1/_2$ cup granulated sugar

1 teaspoon vanilla extract

$^1/_3$ cup granulated sugar

$^1/_2$ cup all-purpose flour

$^1/_3$ cup HERSHEY'S Cocoa

$^1/_4$ teaspoon baking powder

$^1/_4$ teaspoon baking soda

$^1/_8$ teaspoon salt

$^1/_3$ cup water

Powdered sugar

1 can (21 ounces) cherry pie filling, divided

$1^1/_2$ cups whipped topping

Chocolate Glaze (page 54)

1. Heat oven to 375°F. Line $15^1/_2 \times 10^1/_2 \times ^1/_2$-inch jelly-roll pan with foil; generously grease foil.

2. Beat egg whites in large bowl until foamy; gradually add $^1/_2$ cup granulated sugar, beating until stiff peaks form.

3. Beat egg yolks and vanilla in small bowl on high speed for about 3 minutes. Gradually add $^1/_3$ cup granulated sugar; continue beating 2 minutes. Combine flour, cocoa, baking powder, baking soda and salt; add to egg yolk mixture alternately with water on low speed, beating just until batter is smooth.

4. Fold chocolate mixture gradually into egg whites; spread evenly into prepared pan.

continued on page 54

Chocolate Cherry Cream-Filled Log, continued

5. Bake 12 to 15 minutes or until top springs back when touched lightly in center. Immediately loosen cake from edges of pan; invert onto towel sprinkled with powdered sugar. Carefully remove foil. Immediately roll cake in towel starting from narrow end; place on wire rack to cool.

6. Combine 1 cup pie filling and whipped topping; mix well. Unroll cake; remove towel. Spread with filling; reroll cake.

7. Prepare Chocolate Glaze; drizzle over top, allowing to run down sides of cake. Refrigerate several hours. Just before serving, spoon $^1/_2$ cup pie filling over cake. Serve with remaining pie filling.

Makes 10 to 12 servings

Prep Time: 30 minutes
Bake Time: 12 minutes
Cool Time: 1 hour
Chill Time: 3 hours

Chocolate Glaze

> 2 tablespoons butter or margarine
> 2 tablespoons HERSHEY'S Cocoa
> 2 tablespoons water
> 1 cup powdered sugar
> $^1/_2$ teaspoon vanilla extract

1. Melt butter in small saucepan over low heat. Add cocoa and water. Cook, stirring constantly, until smooth and slightly thickened. Do not boil.

2. Remove from heat; cool slightly. Gradually blend in sugar and vanilla.

Reese's Peanut Butter 'n' Chocolate Pie

1$^1/_3$ cups HERSHEY'S MINI KISSES Semi-Sweet *or* Milk
   Chocolate Baking Pieces, divided

2 tablespoons milk

1 packaged crumb crust (6 ounces)

1 package (8 ounces) Neufchâtel cheese ($^1/_3$ less fat), softened

$^3/_4$ cup sugar

1 cup REESE'S Creamy or Crunchy Peanut Butter

3$^1/_2$ cups (8 ounces) frozen non-dairy whipped topping, thawed

1. Place $^2/_3$ cup Mini Kisses and milk in small microwave-safe bowl. Microwave at HIGH (100%) 30 to 45 seconds or just until melted and smooth when stirred; spread evenly onto bottom of crust. Cover; refrigerate.

2. Beat Neufchâtel cheese in medium bowl until smooth; gradually beat in sugar. Stir in peanut butter and whipped topping until blended; spoon evenly into crust over chocolate mixture. Cover; refrigerate until set, at least 4 hours.

3. Place remaining $^2/_3$ cup chocolate pieces around edge of filling just before serving. Serve cold; cover and refrigerate leftover pie.

Makes 8 servings

Prep Time: 20 minutes
Cook Time: 30 seconds
Chill Time: 4 hours

Crunchy-Topped Cocoa Cake

$1^1/_2$ cups all-purpose flour

1 cup sugar

$^1/_4$ cup HERSHEY'S Cocoa

1 teaspoon baking soda

$^1/_2$ teaspoon salt

1 cup water

$^1/_4$ cup plus 2 tablespoons vegetable oil

1 tablespoon white vinegar

1 teaspoon vanilla extract

Broiled Topping (recipe follows)

1. Heat oven to 350°F. Grease and flour 8-inch square baking pan.

2. Stir together flour, sugar, cocoa, baking soda and salt in large bowl. Add water, oil, vinegar and vanilla; beat with spoon or whisk just until batter is smooth and ingredients are well blended. Pour batter into prepared pan.

3. Bake 35 to 40 minutes or until wooden pick inserted in center comes out clean. Meanwhile, prepare Broiled Topping; spread on warm cake. Set oven to broil; place pan about 4 inches from heat. Broil 3 minutes or until top is bubbly and golden brown. Remove from oven. Cool completely in pan on wire rack. *Makes 9 servings*

Prep Time: 20 minutes
Bake Time: 35 minutes
Cool Time: $1^1/_2$ hours

Broiled Topping

$^1/_4$ cup ($^1/_2$ stick) butter or margarine, softened

$^1/_2$ cup packed light brown sugar

$^1/_2$ cup coarsely chopped nuts

$^1/_2$ cup MOUNDS Sweetened Coconut Flakes

3 tablespoons light cream or evaporated milk

Stir together all ingredients in small bowl until well blended.

Makes about 1 cup topping

Crunchy-Topped Cocoa Cake

Fudgey Peanut Butter Chip Brownie Pie

2 eggs

1 teaspoon vanilla extract

1 cup sugar

$^1/_2$ cup (1 stick) butter or margarine, melted

$^1/_2$ cup all-purpose flour

$^1/_3$ cup HERSHEY'S Cocoa

$^1/_4$ teaspoon salt

$^2/_3$ cup REESE'S Peanut Butter Chips

1 packaged butter-flavored crumb crust (6 ounces)

Peanut Butter Sauce (recipe follows)

Vanilla ice cream

1. Heat oven to 350°F.

2. Lightly beat eggs and vanilla in small mixer bowl; blend in sugar and butter. Stir together flour, cocoa and salt. Add to egg mixture; beat until blended. Stir in peanut butter chips. Place crust on baking sheet; pour chocolate mixture into crust.

3. Bake 45 to 50 minutes or until set; cool completely on wire rack. Prepare Peanut Butter Sauce; serve over pie and ice cream.

Makes 8 servings

Peanut Butter Sauce

1 cup REESE'S Peanut Butter Chips

$^1/_3$ cup milk

$^1/_4$ cup whipping cream

$^1/_4$ teaspoon vanilla extract

Combine peanut butter chips, milk and whipping cream in small saucepan over low heat. Cook, stirring constantly, until chips are melted and mixture is smooth. Remove from heat; stir in vanilla. Serve warm.

Spicy Butterscotch Snack Cake

1 cup (2 sticks) butter or margarine, softened
1 cup granulated sugar
2 eggs
$^1/_2$ teaspoon vanilla extract
$^1/_2$ cup applesauce
$2^1/_2$ cups all-purpose flour
$1^1/_2$ to 2 teaspoons ground cinnamon
1 teaspoon baking soda
$^1/_2$ teaspoon salt
$1^2/_3$ cups (10-ounce package) HERSHEY'S Butterscotch Chips
1 cup chopped pecans (optional)
Powdered sugar or frozen non-dairy whipped topping, thawed (optional)

1. Heat oven to 350°F. Lightly grease 13×9-inch baking pan.

2. Beat butter and granulated sugar in large bowl until fluffy. Add eggs and vanilla; beat well. Mix in applesauce. Stir together flour, cinnamon, baking soda and salt; gradually add to butter mixture, beating until well blended. Stir in butterscotch chips and pecans, if desired. Spread into prepared pan.

3. Bake 35 minutes or until wooden pick inserted in center comes out clean. Cool completely in pan. Dust with powdered sugar or serve with whipped topping, if desired. *Makes 12 servings*

Chilled Raspberry Cheesecake

1 1/2 cups vanilla wafer crumbs (about 45 wafers, crushed)

1/3 cup HERSHEY'S Cocoa

1/3 cup powdered sugar

1/3 cup butter or margarine, melted

1 package (10 ounces) frozen raspberries, thawed

1 envelope unflavored gelatin

1/2 cup cold water

1/2 cup boiling water

2 packages (8 ounces each) cream cheese, softened

1/2 cup granulated sugar

1 teaspoon vanilla extract

3 tablespoons seedless red raspberry preserves

Chocolate Whipped Cream (recipe follows)

1. Heat oven to 350°F.

2. Stir together crumbs, cocoa and powdered sugar in medium bowl; stir in melted butter. Press mixture onto bottom and 1 1/2 inches up side of 9-inch springform pan. Bake 10 minutes; cool completely.

3. Purée and strain raspberries; set aside. Sprinkle gelatin over cold water in small bowl; let stand several minutes to soften. Add boiling water; stir until gelatin dissolves completely and mixture is clear. Beat cream cheese, granulated sugar and vanilla in large bowl until smooth. Gradually add raspberry purée and gelatin, mixing thoroughly; pour into prepared crust.

4. Refrigerate several hours or overnight. Loosen cake from side of pan with knife; remove side of pan. Spread raspberry preserves over top. Garnish with Chocolate Whipped Cream. Cover; refrigerate leftovers.

Makes 10 to 12 servings

Chocolate Whipped Cream: Stir together $^1/_2$ cup powdered sugar and $^1/_4$ cup HERSHEY'S Cocoa in medium bowl. Add 1 cup chilled whipping cream and 1 teaspoon vanilla extract; beat until stiff.

Chilled Raspberry Cheesecake

Chocolate Chip Walnut Pie

$^3/_4$ cup packed light brown sugar

$^1/_2$ cup all-purpose flour

$^1/_2$ teaspoon baking powder

$^1/_4$ teaspoon ground cinnamon

2 eggs, slightly beaten

1 cup HERSHEY'S Semi-Sweet Chocolate Chips,
   MINI CHIPS or Milk Chocolate Chips

1 cup coarsely chopped walnuts

1 baked (9-inch) pie crust

   Spiced Cream (recipe follows)

1. Heat oven to 350°F.

2. Combine brown sugar, flour, baking powder and cinnamon in medium bowl. Add eggs; stir until well blended. Add chocolate chips and walnuts. Pour into baked pie crust.

3. Bake 25 to 30 minutes or until lightly browned and set. Serve slightly warm or at room temperature with Spiced Cream. Refrigerate leftovers.

Makes 1 (9-inch) pie

Spiced Cream: Combine $^1/_2$ cup chilled whipping cream, 1 tablespoon powdered sugar, $^1/_4$ teaspoon vanilla extract, $^1/_4$ teaspoon ground cinnamon and dash ground nutmeg in small mixer bowl; beat until stiff.

Peanut Butter Chip Cheesecake

$^1/_3$ cup butter or margarine, melted

1$^1/_4$ cups graham cracker crumbs

$^1/_3$ cup HERSHEY'S Cocoa

$^1/_3$ cup sugar

1 cup REESE'S Peanut Butter Chips

2 packages (8 ounces each) cream cheese, softened

1 can (14 ounces) sweetened condensed milk (not evaporated milk)

4 eggs

1 teaspoon vanilla extract

Whipped cream and chocolate curls or shavings (optional)

1. Heat oven to 300°F.

2. Stir together butter, crumbs, cocoa and sugar in medium bowl; press firmly onto bottom of 9-inch springform pan or 13×9×2-inch baking pan.

3. Place peanut butter chips in small microwave-safe bowl. Microwave at HIGH (100%) 1 minute; stir. If necessary, microwave at HIGH an additional 15 seconds at a time, stirring after each heating, just until chips are melted when stirred. Meanwhile, beat cream cheese until fluffy. Gradually beat in sweetened condensed milk and melted chips until smooth. Add eggs and vanilla; mix well. Pour over crust.

4. Bake 50 to 60 minutes or until cake springs back when touched lightly. Cool to room temperature. Refrigerate. Garnish with whipped cream and chocolate curls, if desired. Cover; refrigerate leftover cheesecake.

Makes 12 servings

Orange Streusel Coffeecake

Cocoa Streusel (recipe follows)
3/4 cup (1 1/2 sticks) butter or margarine, softened
1 cup sugar
3 eggs
1 teaspoon vanilla extract
1/2 cup dairy sour cream
3 cups all-purpose flour
2 teaspoons baking powder
1 teaspoon baking soda
1 cup orange juice
2 teaspoons freshly grated orange peel
1/2 cup orange marmalade or apple jelly

1. Prepare Cocoa Streusel. Heat oven to 350°F. Generously grease 12-cup fluted tube pan.

2. In large bowl, beat butter and sugar until well blended. Add eggs and vanilla; beat well. Add sour cream; beat until blended. Stir together flour, baking powder and baking soda; add alternately with orange juice to butter mixture, beating until well blended. Stir in orange peel.

3. Spread marmalade in bottom of prepared pan; sprinkle half of streusel over marmalade. Pour half of batter into pan, spreading evenly. Sprinkle remaining streusel over batter; spread remaining batter evenly over streusel. Bake about 1 hour or until toothpick inserted in center of cake comes out clean. Loosen cake from side of pan with metal spatula; immediately invert onto serving plate.   *Makes 12 servings*

Cocoa Streusel: Stir together ²/₃ cup packed light brown sugar, ¹/₂ cup chopped walnuts, ¹/₄ cup HERSHEY'S Cocoa and ¹/₂ cup MOUNDS Sweetened Coconut Flakes, if desired.

Orange Streusel Coffeecake

Chocolate Lover's Cheesecake

Graham Crust (recipe follows)

2 packages (8 ounces each) cream cheese, softened

3/4 cup plus 2 tablespoons sugar, divided

1/2 cup HERSHEY'S Cocoa

2 teaspoons vanilla extract, divided

2 eggs

1 cup HERSHEY'S Semi-Sweet Chocolate Chips

1 container (8 ounces) dairy sour cream

1. Prepare Graham Crust. Heat oven to 375°F.

2. Beat cream cheese, 3/4 cup sugar, cocoa and 1 teaspoon vanilla in large mixer bowl on medium speed of electric mixer until smooth. Add eggs; beat until blended. Stir in chocolate chips. Pour into prepared crust.

3. Bake 20 minutes. Remove from oven to wire rack; cool 15 minutes. *Increase oven temperature to 425°F.*

4. Stir together sour cream, remaining 2 tablespoons sugar and remaining 1 teaspoon vanilla in small bowl; stir until smooth. Spread over baked filling.

5. Bake 10 minutes. Remove from oven to wire rack. With knife, immediately loosen cake from side of pan. Cool completely; remove side of pan. Refrigerate several hours or until cold. Cover; refrigerate leftover cheesecake. *Makes 10 to 12 servings*

Graham Crust

1 1/2 cups graham cracker crumbs
1/3 cup sugar
1/3 cup butter or margarine, melted

Stir together crumbs, sugar and butter in medium bowl. Press mixture onto bottom and halfway up side of 9-inch springform pan.

Chocolate Cheesepie

1 package (8 ounces) cream cheese, softened
1 package (3 ounces) cream cheese, softened
3/4 cup sugar
1 teaspoon vanilla extract
1/4 cup HERSHEY'S Cocoa
2 eggs
1/2 cup whipping cream
1 packaged graham cracker crumb crust (6 ounces)
Cherry or peach pie filling or sliced fresh fruit

1. Heat oven to 350°F. Beat cream cheese, sugar and vanilla in large bowl until well blended.

2. Add cocoa; beat until well blended, scraping side of bowl and beaters frequently. Add eggs; beat well. Stir in whipping cream. Pour into crust.

3. Bake 35 to 40 minutes. (Center will be soft but will set upon cooling.) Cool to room temperature. Cover; refrigerate several hours or overnight. Serve with pie filling. Cover; refrigerate leftover pie.

Makes 6 to 8 servings

Hershey's "Perfectly Chocolate" Chocolate Cake

2 cups sugar

1 3/4 cups all-purpose flour

3/4 cup HERSHEY'S Cocoa or HERSHEY'S Dutch Processed Cocoa

1 1/2 teaspoons baking powder

1 1/2 teaspoons baking soda

1 teaspoon salt

2 eggs

1 cup milk

1/2 cup vegetable oil

2 teaspoons vanilla extract

1 cup boiling water

"Perfectly Chocolate" Chocolate Frosting (recipe follows)

1. Heat oven to 350°F. Grease and flour two 9-inch round baking pans.*

2. Stir together sugar, flour, cocoa, baking powder, baking soda and salt in large mixer bowl. Add eggs, milk, oil and vanilla; beat on medium speed of electric mixer 2 minutes. Stir in water. (Batter will be thin.) Pour batter evenly into prepared pans.

3. Bake 30 to 35 minutes or until wooden pick inserted in center comes out clean. Cool 10 minutes; remove from pans to wire racks. Cool completely.

4. Prepare "Perfectly Chocolate" Chocolate Frosting; spread between layers and over top and sides of cake. *Makes 8 to 10 servings*

One 13×9×2-inch baking pan may be substituted for 9-inch round baking pans. Prepare as directed above. Bake 35 to 40 minutes. Cool completely in pan on wire rack. Frost as desired.

"Perfectly Chocolate" Chocolate Frosting

1 stick ($^1/_2$ cup) butter or margarine

$^2/_3$ cup HERSHEY'S Cocoa

3 cups powdered sugar

$^1/_3$ cup milk

1 teaspoon vanilla extract

1. Melt butter. Stir in cocoa. Alternately add powdered sugar and milk, beating to spreading consistency.

2. Add small amount additional milk, if needed. Stir in vanilla.

Makes about 2 cups frosting

Hershey's "Perfectly Chocolate" Chocolate Cake

Strawberry Chiffon Pie

Chocolate Pastry (recipe follows)
1 package (3 ounces) strawberry-flavored gelatin
¾ cup boiling water
1½ cups chopped fresh strawberries
2 cups frozen non-dairy whipped topping, thawed
½ cup HERSHEY'S Semi-Sweet Chocolate Chips
1 teaspoon shortening (do not use butter, margarine, spread or oil)
8 whole strawberries

1. Prepare Chocolate Pastry.

2. Dissolve gelatin in boiling water in medium bowl; cool slightly. Crush strawberries or purée to equal ¾ cup. Stir strawberry purée into gelatin mixture; refrigerate until partially set (consistency of unbeaten egg whites). Fold whipped topping into strawberry mixture. Spoon into prepared crust. Refrigerate 2 to 3 hours or until set.

3. Line tray with wax paper. Place chocolate chips and shortening in small microwave-safe bowl. Microwave at HIGH (100%) 1 minute; stir. If necessary, microwave at HIGH an additional 15 seconds at a time, stirring after each heating, just until chips are melted when stirred. Dip whole strawberries into melted chocolate; place on prepared tray. Refrigerate, uncovered, about 30 minutes or until chocolate is firm. Just before serving, garnish pie with chocolate-covered strawberries. Cover; refrigerate leftover pie.   *Makes 8 servings*

Chocolate Pastry

1 ¼ cups all-purpose flour

¼ cup sugar

3 tablespoons HERSHEY'S Cocoa

¼ teaspoon salt

⅓ cup vegetable oil

3 tablespoons cold water

1. Stir together flour, sugar, cocoa and salt in medium bowl. Place oil in measuring cup; add water. Do not stir. Pour liquid over flour mixture; stir lightly with fork until well blended. (If mixture is too dry, add 1 to 2 teaspoons additional cold water.)

2. With hands, shape mixture into ball. Place between two pieces of wax paper; roll into 12-inch circle. Peel off top sheet of paper. Gently invert pastry over 9-inch pie plate; peel off paper. Fit pastry into pie plate. Fold under extra pastry around edge; flute edge. With fork, prick bottom and side of crust thoroughly. Refrigerate about 30 minutes.

3. Meanwhile, heat oven to 450°F. Bake 10 minutes. Cool completely.

Hot Fudge Pudding Cake

$1^{1}/_{4}$ cups granulated sugar, divided

1 cup all-purpose flour

$^{1}/_{2}$ cup HERSHEY'S Cocoa, divided

2 teaspoons baking powder

$^{1}/_{4}$ teaspoon salt

$^{1}/_{2}$ cup milk

$^{1}/_{3}$ cup butter or margarine, melted

$1^{1}/_{2}$ teaspoons vanilla extract

$^{1}/_{2}$ cup packed light brown sugar

$1^{1}/_{4}$ cups hot water

Whipped topping

1. Heat oven to 350°F.

2. Stir together $^{3}/_{4}$ cup granulated sugar, flour, $^{1}/_{4}$ cup cocoa, baking powder and salt. Stir in milk, butter and vanilla; beat until smooth. Pour batter into ungreased 9-inch square baking pan. Stir together remaining $^{1}/_{2}$ cup granulated sugar, brown sugar and remaining $^{1}/_{4}$ cup cocoa; sprinkle mixture evenly over batter. Pour hot water over top. Do not stir.

3. Bake 35 to 40 minutes or until center is almost set. Let stand 15 minutes; spoon into dessert dishes, spooning sauce from bottom of pan over top. Garnish with whipped topping.   *Makes about 8 servings*

Prep Time: 10 minutes
Bake Time: 35 minutes
Cool Time: 15 minutes

Hot Fudge Pudding Cake

Classic Hershey's Bar Cake

1 cup (2 sticks) butter or margarine, softened
1¼ cups granulated sugar
4 eggs
6 HERSHEY'S Milk Chocolate Bars (1.55 ounces each), melted
2½ cups all-purpose flour
¼ teaspoon baking soda
Dash salt
1 cup buttermilk or sour milk*
½ cup HERSHEY'S Syrup
2 teaspoons vanilla extract
1 cup chopped pecans
Powdered sugar (optional)

*To sour milk: Use 1 tablespoon white vinegar plus milk to equal 1 cup.

1. Heat oven to 350°F. Grease and flour 10-inch tube pan or 12-cup fluted tube pan.

2. Beat butter in large mixer bowl until creamy; gradually add granulated sugar, beating on medium speed of electric mixer until well blended. Add eggs, one at a time, beating well after each addition. Add chocolate; beat until blended.

3. Stir together flour, baking soda and salt; add to chocolate mixture alternately with buttermilk, beating until blended. Add syrup and vanilla; beat until blended. Stir in pecans. Pour batter into prepared pan.

4. Bake 1 hour and 15 minutes or until wooden pick inserted in center of cake comes out clean. Cool 10 minutes; remove from pan to wire rack. Cool completely. Sift powdered sugar over top, if desired.

Makes 12 to 16 servings

Classic Boston Cream Pie

$^1/_3$ cup shortening

1 cup sugar

2 eggs

1 teaspoon vanilla extract

$1^1/_4$ cups all-purpose flour

$1^1/_2$ teaspoons baking powder

$^1/_4$ teaspoon salt

$^3/_4$ cup milk

Rich Filling (page 76)

Dark Cocoa Glaze (page 76)

1. Heat oven to 350°F. Grease and flour 9-inch round baking pan.

2. Beat shortening, sugar, eggs and vanilla in large mixer bowl until fluffy. Stir together flour, baking powder and salt; add alternately with milk to shortening mixture, beating well after each addition. Pour batter into prepared pan.

3. Bake 30 to 35 minutes or until wooden pick inserted in center comes out clean. Cool 10 minutes; remove from pan to wire rack. Cool completely.

4. Prepare Rich Filling. With long serrated knife, cut cake in half horizontally. Place one layer, cut side up, on serving plate; spread with prepared filling. Top with remaining layer, cut side down. Prepare Dark Cocoa Glaze; spread over cake, allowing glaze to run down sides. Refrigerate several hours or until cold. Garnish as desired. Refrigerate leftover pie.   *Makes 8 to 10 servings*

continued on page 76

Classic Boston Cream Pie, continued

Rich Filling

$^1/_3$ cup sugar

2 tablespoons cornstarch

$1^1/_2$ cups milk

2 egg yolks, slightly beaten

1 tablespoon butter or margarine

1 teaspoon vanilla extract

Stir together sugar and cornstarch in medium saucepan; gradually add milk and egg yolks, stirring until blended. Cook over medium heat, stirring constantly, until mixture comes to a boil. Boil 1 minute, stirring constantly. Remove from heat; stir in butter and vanilla. Cover; refrigerate several hours or until cold.

Dark Cocoa Glaze

3 tablespoons water

2 tablespoons butter or margarine

3 tablespoons HERSHEY'S Cocoa

1 cup powdered sugar

$^1/_2$ teaspoon vanilla extract

Heat water and butter in small saucepan over medium heat until mixture comes to a boil; remove from heat. Immediately stir in cocoa. Gradually add powdered sugar and vanilla, beating with whisk until smooth and of desired consistency; cool slightly.

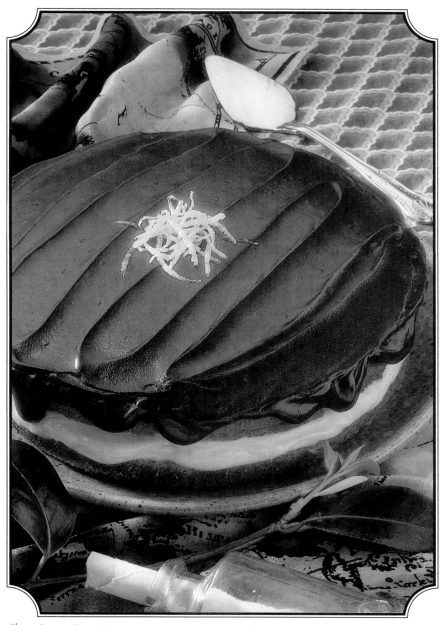

Classic Boston Cream Pie

Easy Rich No-Bake Chocolate Cheesecake

Almond Crumb Crust (recipe follows)
1 package (8 ounces) HERSHEY'S Semi-Sweet Baking
    Chocolate, broken into pieces
3 packages (3 ounces each) cream cheese, softened
$^1/_4$ cup sugar
$^1/_4$ cup ($^1/_2$ stick) butter or margarine, softened
1 teaspoon vanilla extract
1 cup ($^1/_2$ pint) cold whipping cream

1. Prepare Almond Crumb Crust; set aside.

2. Place chocolate in small microwave-safe bowl. Microwave at HIGH (100%) 1 to $1^1/_2$ minutes or until chocolate is melted when stirred. Set aside; cool slightly. Beat cream cheese, sugar, butter and vanilla in large bowl until smooth. Add melted chocolate; beat on low speed of electric mixer.

3. Beat whipping cream in small bowl until stiff; fold into chocolate mixture. Pour mixture into prepared crust. Cover; refrigerate until firm.

Makes about 8 servings

Almond Crumb Crust: Heat oven to 350°F. Stir together 1 cup finely chopped slivered almonds, $^3/_4$ cup vanilla wafer crumbs and $^1/_4$ cup powdered sugar in medium bowl. Pour $^1/_4$ cup ($^1/_2$ stick) melted butter or margarine over crumb mixture; blend well. Press mixture onto bottom and $^1/_2$ inch up side of 9-inch springform pan. Bake 8 to 10 minutes or until lightly browned. Cool completely.

Chocolate Truffle Cake Supreme

1 ¹/₄ cups (2 ¹/₂ sticks) unsalted butter

³/₄ cup HERSHEY'S Cocoa

1 cup plus 1 tablespoon sugar, divided

1 tablespoon all-purpose flour

2 teaspoons vanilla extract

4 eggs, separated

1 cup (¹/₂ pint) cold whipping cream

Chocolate curls (optional)

1. Heat oven to 425°F. Grease bottom of 8-inch springform pan. Melt butter in medium saucepan over low heat. Add cocoa and 1 cup sugar; stir well. Remove from heat; cool. Stir in flour and vanilla. Add egg yolks, one at a time, beating well after each addition. Beat egg whites in medium bowl with remaining 1 tablespoon sugar until soft peaks form; gradually fold into chocolate mixture. Spoon batter into pan.

2. Bake 16 to 18 minutes or until edge is firm (center will be soft). Cool completely on wire rack (cake will sink slightly in center as it cools). Remove side of pan. Refrigerate cake at least 6 hours.

3. Beat whipping cream in small bowl until soft peaks form; spread over top of cake. Cut cake while cold, but let stand at room temperature 10 to 15 minutes before serving. Garnish with chocolate curls, if desired.

Makes 10 servings

Prep Time: 20 minutes
Bake Time: 16 minutes
Cool Time: 1 hour
Chill Time: 6 hours

Take-Me-To-A-Picnic Cake

1 cup water
1 cup (2 sticks) butter or margarine
$^1/_2$ cup HERSHEY'S Cocoa
2 cups sugar
1 $^3/_4$ cups all-purpose flour
1 teaspoon baking soda
$^1/_2$ teaspoon salt
3 eggs
$^3/_4$ cup dairy sour cream
Peanut Butter Chip Frosting (recipe follows)
Chocolate Garnish (recipe follows, optional)

1. Heat oven to 350°F. Grease and flour 15$^1/_2$×10$^1/_2$×1-inch
jelly-roll pan.

2. Combine water, butter and cocoa in medium saucepan. Cook over
medium heat, stirring occasionally, until mixture boils. Boil 1 minute.
Remove from heat. Stir together sugar, flour, baking soda and salt in large
bowl. Add eggs and sour cream; beat until blended. Add cocoa mixture;
beat just until blended. Pour into prepared pan.

3. Bake 25 to 30 minutes or until wooden pick inserted in center comes
out clean. Cool on wire rack. Prepare Peanut Butter Chip Frosting.
Spread over cake. Prepare Chocolate Garnish; drizzle over top, if desired.

Makes about 20 servings

Peanut Butter Chip Frosting: Combine $^1/_3$ cup butter or margarine,
$^1/_3$ cup milk and 1$^2/_3$ cups (10-ounce package) REESE'S Peanut Butter
Chips in medium saucepan. Cook over low heat, stirring constantly,
until chips are melted and mixture is smooth. Remove from heat; stir in

80

1 teaspoon vanilla extract. Place 1 cup powdered sugar in medium bowl. Gradually add chip mixture; beat well. Makes about 2 cups frosting.

Chocolate Garnish: Place ¹/₂ cup HERSHEY'S Semi-Sweet Chocolate Chips and 1 teaspoon shortening (not butter, margarine, spread or oil) in small microwave-safe bowl. Microwave at HIGH (100%) 1 minute; stir until chips are melted and mixture is smooth.

Prep Time: 30 minutes
Bake Time: 25 minutes
Cool Time: 1 hour

Take-Me-To-A-Picnic Cake

Easy Chocolate Cream-Filled Torte

1 frozen pound cake ($10^3/4$ ounces), thawed
$1/2$ cup powdered sugar
$1/4$ cup HERSHEY'S Cocoa
1 cup ($1/2$ pint) cold whipping cream
1 teaspoon vanilla extract
Chocolate Glaze (recipe follows)
Sliced almonds (optional)

1. Cut cake horizontally to make 4 layers. Stir together sugar and cocoa in medium bowl. Add whipping cream and vanilla; beat until stiff.

2. Place bottom cake layer on serving platter. Spread $1/3$ of the whipped cream mixture on cake layer. Place next cake layer on top of whipped cream; continue layering whipped cream mixture and cake until all have been used.

3. Prepare Chocolate Glaze; spoon over top of cake, allowing to drizzle down sides. Garnish with almonds, if desired. Refrigerate until ready to serve. Cover; refrigerate leftover torte. *Makes 8 to 10 servings*

Prep Time: 20 minutes
Chill Time: 30 minutes

Chocolate Glaze

2 tablespoons butter or margarine
2 tablespoons HERSHEY'S Cocoa
2 tablespoons water
1 cup powdered sugar
$1/4$ to $1/2$ teaspoon almond extract

1. Melt butter in small saucepan over low heat. Add cocoa and water. Cook, stirring constantly, until smooth and slightly thickened. Do not boil.

2. Remove from heat. Gradually add powdered sugar and almond extract, beating with whisk until smooth.　　　　　*Makes about ¹/₂ cup glaze*

Easy Chocolate Cream-Filled Torte

Old-Fashioned Chocolate Cake

$^3/_4$ cup ($1^1/_2$ sticks) butter or margarine, softened

$1^2/_3$ cups sugar

3 eggs

1 teaspoon vanilla extract

2 cups all-purpose flour

$^2/_3$ cup HERSHEY'S Cocoa

$1^1/_4$ teaspoons baking soda

1 teaspoon salt

$^1/_4$ teaspoon baking powder

$1^1/_3$ cups water

$^1/_2$ cup finely crushed hard peppermint candy (optional)

One-Bowl Buttercream Frosting (recipe follows)

Additional crushed hard peppermint candy (optional)

1. Heat oven to 350°F. Grease and flour two 9-inch round baking pans or one 13×9×2-inch baking pan.

2. Combine butter, sugar, eggs and vanilla in large mixer bowl; beat on high speed of electric mixer 3 minutes. Stir together flour, cocoa, baking soda, salt and baking powder; add alternately with water to butter mixture. Blend just until combined; add candy, if desired. Pour batter into prepared pans.

3. Bake 30 to 35 minutes or until wooden pick inserted in center comes out clean. Cool 10 minutes; remove from pans to wire racks. Cool completely. Frost with One-Bowl Buttercream Frosting. Just before serving, garnish with peppermint candy, if desired.

Makes 8 to 10 servings

One-Bowl Buttercream Frosting

6 tablespoons butter or margarine, softened

2^2/$_3$ cups powdered sugar

^{1}/$_2$ cup HERSHEY'S Cocoa or HERSHEY'S Dutch Processed
Cocoa

4 to 6 tablespoons milk

1 teaspoon vanilla extract

Beat butter in medium bowl. Add powdered sugar and cocoa alternately
with milk, beating to spreading consistency. Stir in vanilla.

Makes about 2 cups frosting

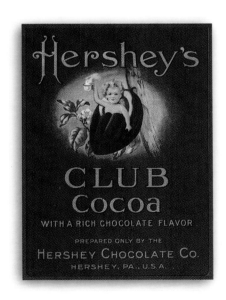

Fudge Truffle Cheesecake

Chocolate Crumb Crust (recipe follows)

2 cups (12-ounce package) HERSHEY'S Semi-Sweet Chocolate Chips

3 packages (8 ounces each) cream cheese, softened

1 can (14 ounces) sweetened condensed milk (not evaporated milk)

4 eggs

2 teaspoons vanilla extract

1. Prepare Chocolate Crumb Crust; set aside. Heat oven to 300°F.

2. Place chocolate chips in microwave-safe bowl. Microwave at HIGH (100%) $1^1/_2$ minutes; stir. If necessary, microwave at HIGH an additional 15 seconds at a time, stirring after each heating, just until chips are melted when stirred.

3. Beat cream cheese in large bowl until fluffy. Gradually beat in sweetened condensed milk until smooth. Add melted chips, eggs and vanilla; mix well. Pour into prepared crust.

4. Bake 1 hour and 5 minutes or until center is set. Remove from oven to wire rack. With knife, loosen cake from side of pan. Cool completely; remove side of pan. Refrigerate several hours before serving. Garnish as desired. Cover; refrigerate leftover cheesecake.

Makes 10 to 12 servings

Chocolate Crumb Crust: Stir together $1^1/_2$ cups vanilla wafer crumbs, $^1/_2$ cup powdered sugar, $^1/_3$ cup HERSHEY'S Cocoa and $^1/_3$ cup melted butter or margarine in bowl. Press firmly onto bottom of 9-inch springform pan.

Fudge Truffle Cheesecake

Our Gal Sundae Pie

Macaroon-Nut Crust (recipe follows)

$^2/_3$ cup packed light brown sugar

3 tablespoons all-purpose flour

2 tablespoons cornstarch

$^1/_2$ teaspoon salt

$2^1/_4$ cups milk

$^1/_2$ cup HERSHEY'S Syrup

3 egg yolks, well beaten

2 tablespoons butter (do not use margarine)

1 teaspoon vanilla extract

Sweetened whipped cream (optional)

Maraschino cherries (optional)

1 HERSHEY'S Milk Chocolate Bar (1.55 ounces), broken into
  pieces (optional)

1. Prepare Macaroon-Nut Crust.

2. Stir together brown sugar, flour, cornstarch and salt in medium
saucepan. Gradually stir in milk, syrup and egg yolks until blended. Cook
over medium heat, stirring constantly, until mixture comes to a boil; boil
1 minute, stirring constantly. Remove from heat; stir in butter and vanilla.
Pour mixture into prepared crust. Press plastic wrap directly onto surface.
Cool on wire rack; refrigerate at least 6 hours.

3. Just before serving, garnish with sweetened whipped cream, maraschino
cherries and chocolate bar pieces, if desired. Cover; refrigerate leftover pie.

Makes 8 servings

Macaroon-Nut Crust

1 ¼ cups coconut macaroon cookie crumbs (use purchased hard
      coconut macaroon cookies)
½ cup chopped walnuts
¼ cup (½ stick) butter (do not use margarine), melted

1. Heat oven to 350°F.

2. Stir together cookie crumbs, walnuts and butter in medium bowl. Press firmly onto bottom and up side of 9-inch pie plate. Bake 8 to 10 minutes or until lightly browned. Cool completely.

Chocolate Raspberry Pound Cake

1 cup seedless black raspberry preserves,* divided

2 cups all-purpose flour

1 1/2 cups granulated sugar

3/4 cup HERSHEY'S Cocoa

1 1/2 teaspoons baking soda

1 teaspoon salt

2/3 cup butter or margarine, softened

1 container (16 ounces) dairy sour cream

2 eggs

1 teaspoon vanilla extract

Powdered sugar

Raspberry Cream (recipe follows)

Red raspberry jam may be substituted.

1. Heat oven to 350°F. Grease and flour 12-cup fluted tube pan.

2. Place 3/4 cup preserves in small microwave-safe bowl. Microwave at HIGH (100%) 30 to 45 seconds or until melted; cool. Stir together flour, granulated sugar, cocoa, baking soda and salt in large bowl. Add butter, sour cream, eggs, vanilla and melted preserves; beat on medium speed of electric mixer 3 to 4 minutes until well blended. Pour batter into prepared pan.

3. Bake 50 to 60 minutes or until wooden pick inserted in center comes out clean. Cool 10 minutes; remove from pan to wire rack. Place remaining 1/4 cup preserves in small microwave-safe bowl. Microwave at HIGH 30 seconds or until melted; brush over warm cake. Cool completely.

4. At serving time, sprinkle powdered sugar over top. Prepare Raspberry Cream; fill cavity with cream. Garnish, if desired.

Makes about 12 servings

Raspberry Cream: Thaw 1 package (10 ounces) frozen red raspberries in light syrup. Purée in food processor or blender. Strain into medium bowl; discard seeds. Blend 3½ cups (8 ounces) frozen non-dairy whipped topping, thawed, with raspberry purée. Stir in 2 tablespoons raspberry-flavored liqueur, if desired.

Prep Time: 35 minutes
Bake Time: 50 minutes
Cool Time: 3 hours

Chocolate Raspberry Pound Cake

Decadent Desserts

When you want to impress your guests, all it takes is a fabulous chocolate dessert. Try a mousse, soufflé, cream puffs or crêpes—the hardest part is deciding what to make!

Strawberry Chocolate Chip Shortcake

1 cup sugar, divided

$^1/_2$ cup (1 stick) butter or margarine, softened

1 egg

2 teaspoons vanilla extract, divided

1$^1/_2$ cups all-purpose flour

$^1/_2$ teaspoon baking powder

1 cup HERSHEY'S MINI CHIPS Semi-Sweet Chocolate or
      HERSHEY'S Semi-Sweet Chocolate Chips, divided

2 cups dairy sour cream

2 eggs

2 cups frozen non-dairy whipped topping, thawed
      Fresh strawberries, rinsed and halved

1. Heat oven to 350°F. Grease 9-inch springform pan.

2. Beat $^1/_2$ cup sugar and butter in large bowl. Add 1 egg and 1 teaspoon vanilla; beat until creamy. Gradually add flour and baking powder, beating until smooth; stir in $^1/_2$ cup small chocolate chips. Press mixture onto bottom of prepared pan.

3. Stir together sour cream, remaining $^1/_2$ cup sugar, 2 eggs and remaining 1 teaspoon vanilla in medium bowl; stir in remaining $^1/_2$ cup small chocolate chips. Pour over mixture in pan.

4. Bake 50 to 55 minutes until almost set in center and edges are lightly browned. Cool completely on wire rack; remove side of pan. Spread whipped topping over top. Cover; refrigerate. Just before serving, arrange strawberry halves on top of cake; garnish as desired. Refrigerate leftover dessert.   *Makes 12 servings*

Two Great Tastes Pudding Parfaits

1 package (6-serving size, 4.6 ounces) vanilla cook & serve
     pudding and pie filling mix*
3 1/2 cups milk
1 cup REESE'S Peanut Butter Chips
1 cup HERSHEY'S Semi-Sweet or Milk Chocolate MINI
     KISSES Baking Pieces
Whipped topping (optional)
Additional MINI KISSES or grated chocolate

Do not use instant pudding mix.

1. Combine pudding mix and 3 1/2 cups milk in large heavy saucepan (rather than amount listed in package directions). Cook over medium heat, stirring constantly, until mixture comes to a full boil. Remove from heat; divide hot mixture between 2 heat-proof medium bowls.

2. Immediately stir peanut butter chips into mixture in one bowl and MINI KISSES into second bowl. Stir both mixtures until chips are melted and mixture is smooth. Cool slightly, stirring occasionally.

3. Alternately layer peanut butter and chocolate mixtures in parfait dishes, wine glasses or dessert dishes. Place plastic wrap directly onto surface of each dessert; refrigerate about 6 hours. Garnish with whipped topping, if desired, and MINI KISSES. *Makes 4 to 6 servings*

Two Great Tastes Pudding Parfaits

Napoleons

1 package (17¹/₄ ounces) frozen puff pastry sheets
Chocolate Filling (recipe follows)
Vanilla Glaze (recipe follows)
Chocolate Glaze (recipe follows)

1. Thaw folded pastry sheets as package directs. Heat oven to 350°F. Gently unfold sheets. On lightly floured surface, roll each sheet to 15×12-inch rectangle; trim to even edges. Place on large ungreased baking sheets; prick each sheet thoroughly with fork. Bake 18 to 20 minutes or until puffed and golden brown. Cool completely on baking sheets.

2. Prepare Chocolate Filling.

3. Cut one rectangle lengthwise into 3 equal pieces. Place one piece on serving plate; spread with one fourth of the Chocolate Filling. Top with second piece of pastry; spread with one fourth of the filling. Place remaining piece on top; set aside. Repeat with remaining pastry and filling.

4. Prepare Vanilla Glaze; spread onto top of each pastry. Prepare Chocolate Glaze; drizzle over Vanilla Glaze in decorative design. Refrigerate at least 1 hour or until filling is set. Carefully cut each pastry into 6 pieces. Cover; refrigerate leftovers. *Makes 12 servings*

Chocolate Filling

> 1 envelope unflavored gelatin
> 2 tablespoons cold water
> $^1/_4$ cup boiling water
> 1 cup sugar
> $^1/_2$ cup HERSHEY'S Cocoa
> 2 cups (1 pint) cold whipping cream
> 2 teaspoons vanilla extract

1. Sprinkle gelatin over cold water in small bowl; let stand 1 minute to soften. Add boiling water; stir until gelatin is completely dissolved and mixture is clear. Cool slightly.

2. Stir together sugar and cocoa in large mixer bowl. Add whipping cream and vanilla; beat at medium speed, scraping bottom of bowl occasionally, until stiff. Add gelatin mixture; beat until well blended. Refrigerate to spreading consistency, if necessary. *Makes about 5 cups*

Vanilla Glaze: In small mixer bowl, combine $1^1/_2$ cups powdered sugar, 1 tablespoon light corn syrup, $^1/_4$ teaspoon vanilla extract and 1 to 2 tablespoons hot water; beat to spreading consistency. (Add additional water, $^1/_2$ teaspoon at a time, if necessary.)

Chocolate Glaze: In small saucepan, melt $^1/_4$ cup butter or margarine. Remove from heat; stir in $^1/_3$ cup HERSHEY'S Cocoa until smooth. Cool slightly.

Cocoa Cappuccino Mousse

1 can (14 ounces) sweetened condensed milk (not evaporated milk)
$1/3$ cup HERSHEY'S Cocoa
3 tablespoons butter or margarine
2 teaspoons powdered instant coffee or espresso, dissolved
    in 2 teaspoons hot water
2 cups (1 pint) cold whipping cream

1. Combine sweetened condensed milk, cocoa, butter and coffee in medium saucepan. Cook over low heat, stirring constantly, until butter melts and mixture is smooth. Remove from heat; cool.

2. Beat whipping cream in large bowl until stiff. Gradually fold chocolate mixture into whipped cream. Spoon into dessert dishes. Refrigerate until set, about 2 hours. Garnish as desired.   *Makes 8 servings*

Prep Time: 15 minutes
Cook Time: 10 minutes
Chill Time: 2 hours

Cocoa Cappuccino Mousse

Hot Chocolate Soufflé

³/₄ cup HERSHEY'S Cocoa

1 cup sugar, divided

¹/₂ cup all-purpose flour

¹/₄ teaspoon salt

2 cups milk

6 egg yolks, well beaten

2 tablespoons butter or margarine

1 teaspoon vanilla extract

8 egg whites

¹/₄ teaspoon cream of tartar

Sweetened whipped cream

1. Adjust oven rack to lowest position. Heat oven to 350°F. Lightly butter 2¹/₂-quart soufflé dish; sprinkle with sugar. For collar, cut a length of heavy-duty aluminum foil to fit around soufflé dish; fold in thirds lengthwise. Lightly butter one side. Attach foil, buttered side in, around outside of dish, allowing foil to extend at least 2 inches above dish. Secure foil with tape or string.

2. Stir together cocoa, ³/₄ cup sugar, flour and salt in large saucepan; gradually stir in milk. Cook over medium heat, stirring constantly with wire whisk, until mixture boils; remove from heat. Gradually stir small amount of chocolate mixture into beaten egg yolks; blend well. Add egg mixture to chocolate mixture in pan, blending well. Cook and stir 1 minute. Add butter and vanilla, stirring until blended. Set aside; cool 20 minutes.

3. Beat egg whites with cream of tartar in large bowl until soft peaks form; gradually add remaining ¹/₄ cup sugar, beating until stiff peaks form. Gently fold about one-third of beaten egg white mixture into chocolate

mixture. Lightly fold chocolate mixture, half at a time, into remaining beaten egg white mixture just until blended; do not overfold.

4. Gently pour mixture into prepared dish; smooth top with spatula. Gently place dish in larger baking pan; pour hot water into larger pan to depth of 1 inch.

5. Bake 65 to 70 minutes or until puffed and set. Remove soufflé dish from water. Carefully remove foil. Serve immediately with sweetened whipped cream.   *Makes 8 to 10 servings*

Hot Chocolate Soufflé

Cocoa Black Forest Crêpes

3 eggs

$^3/_4$ cup water

$^1/_2$ cup light cream or half-and-half

$^3/_4$ cup plus 2 tablespoons all-purpose flour

3 tablespoons HERSHEY'S Cocoa

2 tablespoons sugar

$^1/_8$ teaspoon salt

3 tablespoons butter or margarine, melted and cooled

Cherry pie filling

Chocolate Sauce (recipe follows)

Sweetened whipped cream (optional)

1. Combine eggs, water and light cream in blender or food processor; blend 10 seconds. Add flour, cocoa, sugar, salt and butter; blend until smooth. Let stand at room temperature 30 minutes.

2. Spray 6-inch crêpe pan lightly with vegetable cooking spray; heat over medium heat. For each crêpe, pour 2 to 3 tablespoons batter into pan; lift and tilt pan to spread batter. Return to heat; cook until surface begins to dry. Loosen crêpe around edges; turn and lightly cook other side. Stack crêpes, placing wax paper between crêpes. Keep covered. (Refrigerate for later use, if desired.)

3. Just before serving, place 2 tablespoons pie filling onto each crêpe; roll up. Place crêpes on dessert plate. Prepare Chocolate Sauce; spoon over crêpes. Garnish with sweetened whipped cream, if desired.

Makes about 18 crêpes

Chocolate Sauce

$^3/_4$ cup sugar

$^1/_3$ cup HERSHEY'S Cocoa

$^3/_4$ cup evaporated milk

$^1/_4$ cup ($^1/_2$ stick) butter or margarine

$^1/_8$ teaspoon salt

1 teaspoon kirsch (cherry brandy, optional)

Stir together sugar and cocoa in small saucepan; blend in evaporated milk, butter and salt. Cook over medium heat, stirring constantly, until mixture comes to a boil. Remove from heat; stir in kirsch, if desired. Serve warm. Cover; refrigerate leftover sauce.

Mini Chocolate Pies

1 package (4-serving size) chocolate cook & serve pudding and pie
    filling mix*
1 cup HERSHEY'S MINI CHIPS Semi-Sweet Chocolate
1 package (4 ounces) single serve graham cracker crusts (6 crusts)
    Whipped topping
    Additional MINI CHIPS Semi-Sweet Chocolate

Do not use instant pudding mix.

1. Prepare pudding and pie filling mix as directed on package; remove
from heat. Immediately add 1 cup small chocolate chips; stir until melted.
Cool 5 minutes, stirring occasionally.

2. Pour filling into crusts; press plastic wrap directly onto surface.
Refrigerate several hours or until firm. Garnish with whipped topping and
small chocolate chips.   *Makes 6 servings*

Prep Time: 5 minutes
Cook Time: 10 minutes
Cool Time: 5 minutes
Chill Time: 2 hours

Mini Chocolate Pies

Chocolate-Filled Cream Puffs

1 cup water
¹/₂ cup (1 stick) butter or margarine
¹/₄ teaspoon salt
1 cup all-purpose flour
4 eggs
Chocolate Cream Filling (recipe follows)
Powdered sugar

1. Heat oven to 400°F.

2. Bring water, butter and salt to a boil in medium saucepan. Add flour; stir vigorously over low heat about 1 minute or until mixture leaves side of pan and forms a ball. Remove from heat; add eggs, one at a time, beating well after each addition until smooth and velvety.

3. Drop dough by scant ¹/₄ cupfuls onto ungreased cookie sheet. Bake 35 to 40 minutes or until puffed and golden brown. While still warm, horizontally slice off small portion of tops; reserve. Remove any soft dough inside; cool.

4. Prepare Chocolate Cream Filling; fill cream puffs. Replace tops; dust with powdered sugar. Chill.   *Makes about 12 cream puffs*

Miniature Cream Puffs: Drop cream puff dough by level teaspoons onto ungreased cookie sheet. Bake at 400°F about 15 minutes. Fill as directed. Makes about 8 dozen miniature cream puffs.

Chocolate Cream Filling

1¼ cups granulated sugar

⅓ cup HERSHEY'S Cocoa

⅓ cup cornstarch

¼ teaspoon salt

3 cups milk

3 egg yolks, slightly beaten

2 tablespoons butter or margarine

1½ teaspoons vanilla extract

Combine granulated sugar, cocoa, cornstarch and salt in medium saucepan; stir in milk. Cook over medium heat, stirring constantly, until mixture boils; boil and stir 1 minute. Remove from heat. Gradually stir small amount of chocolate mixture into egg yolks; blend well. Return egg mixture to chocolate mixture in pan; stir and heat just until boiling. Remove from heat; blend in 2 tablespoons butter and vanilla. Pour into bowl; press plastic wrap directly onto surface. Cool.

Tantalizing Treats

No need to wait for a holiday or a special occasion—truffles, fudge and other intensely chocolatey treasures are simple to make and can brighten up any day.

Creamy Double Decker Fudge

1 cup REESE'S Peanut Butter Chips
1 can (14 ounces) sweetened condensed milk (not evaporated
   milk), divided
1 teaspoon vanilla extract, divided
1 cup HERSHEY'S Semi-Sweet Chocolate Chips

1. Line 8-inch square pan with foil.

2. Place peanut butter chips and $2/3$ cup sweetened condensed milk in small microwave-safe bowl. Microwave at HIGH (100%) 1 to $1\frac{1}{2}$ minutes, stirring after 1 minute, until chips are melted and mixture is smooth when stirred. Stir in $1/2$ teaspoon vanilla; spread evenly into prepared pan.

3. Place remaining sweetened condensed milk and chocolate chips in another small microwave-safe bowl; repeat above microwave procedure. Stir in remaining $1/2$ teaspoon vanilla; spread evenly over peanut butter layer.

4. Cover; refrigerate until firm. Remove from pan; place on cutting board. Peel off foil. Cut into squares. Store tightly covered in refrigerator.

Makes about 4 dozen pieces or $1\frac{1}{2}$ pounds

Note: For best results, do not double this recipe.

Prep Time: 15 minutes
Cook Time: 3 minutes
Chill Time: 2 hours

Butter Almond Crunch

1 1/2 cups HERSHEY'S Semi-Sweet Chocolate Chips, divided
1 3/4 cups chopped almonds, divided
1 1/2 cups (3 sticks) butter or margarine
1 3/4 cups sugar
    3 tablespoons light corn syrup
    3 tablespoons water

1. Heat oven to 350°F. Line 13×9×2-inch pan with foil; butter foil.

2. Sprinkle 1 cup chocolate chips into pan; set aside. Spread chopped almonds in shallow baking dish. Bake about 7 minutes or until golden brown; set aside.

3. Melt butter in heavy 3-quart saucepan; blend in sugar, corn syrup and water. Cook over medium heat, stirring constantly, to 300°F on a candy thermometer (hard-crack stage) or until mixture separates into hard, brittle threads when dropped into very cold water. (Bulb of candy thermometer should not rest on bottom of saucepan.) Remove from heat; stir in 1 1/2 cups toasted almonds. Immediately spread mixture evenly over chocolate chips in prepared pan; do not disturb chips. Sprinkle with remaining 1/4 cup toasted almonds and remaining 1/2 cup chocolate chips; cool slightly.

4. Score candy into 1 1/2-inch squares with sharp knife, wiping knife blade after drawing through candy. Cool completely; remove from pan. Remove foil; break candy into pieces. Store in airtight container in cool, dry place.

Makes about 2 pounds candy

Butter Almond Crunch

Luscious Cocoa Smoothies

1/4 cup HERSHEY'S Cocoa

2 tablespoons sugar

3 tablespoons warm water

1 banana, peeled and sliced

1 1/2 cups skim milk

2 cups nonfat frozen yogurt

Stir together cocoa and sugar in small bowl. Add water; stir until well blended. In blender, place banana and cocoa mixture. Cover; blend until smooth. Add milk and frozen yogurt. Cover; blend until smooth. Serve immediately.   *Makes 4 servings*

Royal Hot Chocolate

2 bars (1 ounce each) HERSHEY'S Unsweetened Baking
    Chocolate, broken into pieces

1 can (14 ounces) sweetened condensed milk (not evaporated milk)

4 cups boiling water

1 teaspoon vanilla extract

Dash salt

Whipped cream (optional)

Ground cinnamon (optional)

Melt chocolate in large heavy saucepan over low heat. Stir in sweetened condensed milk. Gradually add water, stirring until well blended. Stir in vanilla and salt. Garnish with whipped cream and cinnamon, if desired. Serve immediately.   *Makes 8 servings*

Mocha Shake

$^{1}/_{4}$ cup warm water

2 tablespoons HERSHEY'S Cocoa

1 tablespoon sugar

1 to 2 teaspoons powdered instant coffee

$^{1}/_{2}$ cup milk

2 cups vanilla ice cream

Place water, cocoa, sugar and instant coffee in blender container. Cover; blend briefly on low speed. Add milk. Cover; blend well on high speed. Add ice cream. Cover; blend until smooth. Serve immediately. Garnish as desired.

Makes 3 servings

Left to right: Royal Hot Chocolate, Mocha Shake and Luscious Cocoa Smoothie

Double Chocolate Truffles

$^{1}/_{2}$ cup whipping cream

1 tablespoon butter or margarine

4 bars (1 ounce each) HERSHEY'S Semi-Sweet Baking
   Chocolate, broken into pieces

1 HERSHEY'S Milk Chocolate Bar (7 ounces), broken into
   pieces

1 tablespoon amaretto (almond-flavored liqueur) *or* $^{1}/_{4}$ to
   $^{1}/_{2}$ teaspoon almond extract

Ground almonds

1. Combine whipping cream and butter in small saucepan. Cook over medium heat, stirring constantly, just until mixture is very hot. Do not boil. Remove from heat; add chocolate, chocolate bar pieces and liqueur. Stir with whisk until smooth.

2. Press plastic wrap directly onto surface; cool several hours or until mixture is firm enough to handle. Shape into 1-inch balls; roll in almonds to coat. Refrigerate until firm, about 2 hours. Store in tightly covered container in refrigerator.   *Makes about 2 dozen candies*

Quick Creamy Chocolate Pudding

$^2/_3$ cup sugar

$^1/_4$ cup HERSHEY'S Cocoa

3 tablespoons cornstarch

$^1/_4$ teaspoon salt

$2^1/_4$ cups milk

2 tablespoons butter or margarine

1 teaspoon vanilla extract

Whipped topping (optional)

Chopped nuts (optional)

1. Stir together sugar, cocoa, cornstarch and salt in medium saucepan; gradually stir in milk. Cook over medium heat, stirring constantly, until mixture boils; boil and stir 1 minute. Remove from heat; stir in butter and vanilla.

2. Pour into individual dessert dishes. Press plastic wrap directly onto surface; refrigerate. Remove plastic wrap. Garnish with whipped topping and nuts, if desired. *Makes 4 to 5 servings*

Microwave Directions: Stir together sugar, cocoa, cornstarch and salt in large microwave-safe bowl; gradually stir in milk. Microwave at HIGH (100%) 7 to 10 minutes or until mixture comes to a full boil, stirring every 2 minutes. Stir in butter and vanilla. Proceed as directed above.

Cashew Macadamia Crunch

2 cups (11.5-ounce package) HERSHEY'S Milk Chocolate Chips

¾ cup coarsely chopped salted or unsalted cashews

¾ cup coarsely chopped salted or unsalted macadamia nuts

½ cup (1 stick) butter, softened

½ cup sugar

2 tablespoons light corn syrup

1. Line 9-inch square pan with foil, extending foil over edges of pan. Butter foil. Cover bottom of prepared pan with chocolate chips.

2. Combine cashews, macadamia nuts, butter, sugar and corn syrup in large heavy skillet; cook over low heat, stirring constantly, until butter is melted and sugar is dissolved. Increase heat to medium; cook, stirring constantly, until mixture begins to cling together and turns golden brown.

3. Pour mixture over chocolate chips in pan, spreading evenly. Cool. Refrigerate until chocolate is firm. Remove from pan; peel off foil. Break into pieces. Store, tightly covered in cool, dry place.

Makes about 1½ pounds candy

Prep Time: 30 minutes

Cook Time: 10 minutes

Cool Time: 40 minutes

Chill Time: 3 hours

Cashew Macadamia Crunch

Chocolate & Peanut Butter Dipped Apples

10 to 12 medium apples, stems removed
10 to 12 wooden ice cream sticks
1 cup HERSHEY'S Semi-Sweet Chocolate Chips
1²/₃ cups (10-ounce package) REESE'S Peanut Butter Chips, divided
¹/₄ cup plus 2 tablespoons shortening (do not use butter, margarine, spread or oil), divided

1. Line tray with wax paper. Wash apples; dry thoroughly. Insert wooden stick into each apple; place on prepared tray.

2. Place chocolate chips, ²/₃ cup peanut butter chips and ¹/₄ cup shortening in medium microwave-safe bowl. Microwave at HIGH (100%) 1 minute; stir. If necessary, microwave at HIGH an additional 30 seconds at a time, stirring after each heating, just until chips are melted when stirred. Dip bottom three-fourths of each apple into mixture. Twirl and gently shake to remove excess; return to prepared tray.

3. Place remaining 1 cup peanut butter chips and remaining 2 tablespoons shortening in small microwave-safe bowl. Microwave at HIGH 30 seconds; stir. If necessary, microwave at HIGH an additional 15 seconds at a time, stirring after each heating, just until chips are melted when stirred. Spoon over top section of each apple, allowing to drip down sides. Store in refrigerator. *Makes 10 to 12 coated apples*

Chocolate & Peanut Butter Dipped Apples

Crunchy Nutty Ice Cream Sundaes

Peanut Butter Sauce (recipe follows)
Coconut Crunch (recipe follows)
1 pint vanilla ice cream

Prepare Peanut Butter Sauce and Coconut Crunch. Spoon sauce over scoops of ice cream; sprinkle crunch over top. Serve immediately.

Makes 4 sundaes

Peanut Butter Sauce: Melt 1 cup REESE'S Peanut Butter Chips with $^1/_3$ cup milk and $^1/_4$ cup whipping cream in medium saucepan over low heat, stirring constantly, until chips are melted. Remove form heat; stir in $^1/_4$ teaspoon vanilla extract. Cool to room temperature. Makes 1 cup sauce.

Coconut Crunch: Heat oven to 325°F. Combine $^1/_2$ cup MOUNDS Sweetened Coconut Flakes, $^1/_2$ cup chopped nuts and 1 tablespoon butter or margarine in shallow baking pan. Toast in oven, stirring occasionally, 6 to 8 minutes or until butter is melted and mixture is very lightly browned. (Watch carefully so mixture does not burn.) Cool to room temperature. Makes about 1 cup.

Top to bottom: Crunchy Nutty Ice Cream Sundae, Cocoa Black Forest Crêpes (page 102)

Chocolate Coconut Balls

3 bars (1 ounce each) HERSHEY'S Unsweetened Baking
Chocolate
$^1/_4$ cup ($^1/_2$ stick) butter
$^1/_2$ cup sweetened condensed milk (not evaporated milk)
$^3/_4$ cup granulated sugar
$^1/_4$ cup water
1 tablespoon light corn syrup
1 teaspoon vanilla extract
2 cups MOUNDS Sweetened Coconut Flakes
1 cup chopped nuts
Powdered sugar

1. Melt chocolate and butter in large heavy saucepan over very low heat.
Add sweetened condensed milk; stir to blend. Remove from heat.

2. Stir together granulated sugar, water and corn syrup in small saucepan.
Cook over medium heat, stirring constantly, until sugar is dissolved. Cook,
without stirring, until mixture reaches 250°F on candy thermometer or
until a small amount of syrup, when dropped into very cold water, forms a
firm ball which does not flatten when removed from water. (Bulb of candy
thermometer should not rest on bottom of saucepan.) Remove from heat;
stir into chocolate mixture. Add vanilla, coconut and nuts; stir until well
blended.

3. Refrigerate about 30 minutes or until firm enough to handle. Shape
into 1-inch balls; roll in powdered sugar. Store tightly covered in cool, dry
place. *Makes about 4 dozen candies*

Note: For best results, do not double this recipe.

VOLUME MEASUREMENTS (dry)

$^1/_8$ teaspoon = 0.5 mL
$^1/_4$ teaspoon = 1 mL
$^1/_2$ teaspoon = 2 mL
$^3/_4$ teaspoon = 4 mL
1 teaspoon = 5 mL
1 tablespoon = 15 mL
2 tablespoons = 30 mL
$^1/_4$ cup = 60 mL
$^1/_3$ cup = 75 mL
$^1/_2$ cup = 125 mL
$^2/_3$ cup = 150 mL
$^3/_4$ cup = 175 mL
1 cup = 250 mL
2 cups = 1 pint = 500 mL
3 cups = 750 mL
4 cups = 1 quart = 1 L

VOLUME MEASUREMENTS (fluid)

1 fluid ounce (2 tablespoons) = 30 mL
4 fluid ounces ($^1/_2$ cup) = 125 mL
8 fluid ounces (1 cup) = 250 mL
12 fluid ounces (1$^1/_2$ cups) = 375 mL
16 fluid ounces (2 cups) = 500 mL

WEIGHTS (mass)

$^1/_2$ ounce = 15 g
1 ounce = 30 g
3 ounces = 90 g
4 ounces = 120 g
8 ounces = 225 g
10 ounces = 285 g
12 ounces = 360 g
16 ounces = 1 pound = 450 g

DIMENSIONS

$^1/_{16}$ inch = 2 mm
$^1/_8$ inch = 3 mm
$^1/_4$ inch = 6 mm
$^1/_2$ inch = 1.5 cm
$^3/_4$ inch = 2 cm
1 inch = 2.5 cm

OVEN TEMPERATURES

250°F = 120°C
275°F = 140°C
300°F = 150°C
325°F = 160°C
350°F = 180°C
375°F = 190°C
400°F = 200°C
425°F = 220°C
450°F = 230°C

BAKING PAN SIZES

Utensil	Size in Inches/Quarts	Metric Volume	Size in Centimeters
Baking or	8×8×2	2 L	20×20×5
Cake Pan	9×9×2	2.5 L	23×23×5
(square or	12×8×2	3 L	30×20×5
rectangular)	13×9×2	3.5 L	33×23×5
Loaf Pan	8×4×3	1.5 L	20×10×7
	9×5×3	2 L	23×13×7
Round Layer	8×1½	1.2 L	20×4
Cake Pan	9×1½	1.5 L	23×4
Pie Plate	8×1¼	750 mL	20×3
	9×1¼	1 L	23×3
Baking Dish	1 quart	1 L	—
or Casserole	1½ quart	1.5 L	—
	2 quart	2 L	—